EXPLORING VARIOUS BRANCHES OF ASTRONOMY

AN INTRODUCTION TO BRANCHES OF ASTRONOMY FOR BEGINNERS

KANCHANA MUNIRATHNAM

To my beloved husband Vinodh and son
Vedatman Thiruvadi

Contents

Preface

One of the oldest natural sciences is astronomy. The night sky was meticulously observed by early civilizations in recorded history.

Babylonians, Greeks, Indians, Egyptians, Chinese, Maya, and many more ancient indigenous peoples of the Americas are among them.Observational and theoretical astronomy are the two fields of professional astronomy.

Astronomy is a broad science that encompasses a number of sub-fields centred on the study of various aspects of the universe. If you're interested in pursuing a career in astronomy and want to learn more about different branches of the subject, this book will provide you a overview.

> "*We are made of stellar ash. Our origin and evolution have been tied to distant cosmic events. The exploration of the cosmos is a voyage of self-discovery.*"
> *— Carl Sagan, Cosmos*"

OBSERVATIONAL ASTRONOMY

CHAPTER ONE

OBSERVATIONAL ASTRONOMY

Observational Astronomy is the practise and study of observing celestial objects using telescopes and other astronomical instruments.In contrast to theoretical astronomy,which is primarily concerned with calculating the measurable consequences of physical models, observational astronomy is focused with recording data about the observable universe.

Optical telescopes were used to perform practically all observations in the visual spectrum during much of the history of observational astronomy. While the Earth's atmosphere is relatively transparent in this part of the electromagnetic spectrum, most telescope work is still limited to night time due to viewing conditions and air transparency.

Astronomers can make measurements of the skies using a variety of observational instruments. Direct and highly exact position measurements against a more distant and so almost stationary backdrop can be achieved for objects that are relatively close to the Sun and Earth.

Astronomers have increasingly been able to obtain information in different parts of the electromagnetic spectrum in addition to examining the universe in the optical spectrum.Divisions of observational astronomy is based on the region of the electromagnetic spectrum observed.

Optical astronomy is the branch of astronomy that studies light from near-infrared to near-ultraviolet wavelengths using optical instruments (mirrors, lenses, and solid-state detectors). In the middle of this spectrum is visible-light astronomy, which uses wavelengths measurable by the human eye (about 400–700 nm).

Infrared astronomy is concerned with the detection and analysis of infrared radiation with wavelengths greater than the detection limit of silicon solid-state detectors, which is roughly 1 m. The most popular equipment is a reflecting telescope equipped with an infrared-sensitive detector. At some wavelengths, when the atmosphere is opaque, or to minimise noise caused by thermal radiation from the atmosphere, space telescopes are used.

Radio astronomy detects radiation with wavelengths ranging from millimetres to decametres. The receivers are comparable to those used in radio broadcasting, but they are far more sensitive.Radio astronomy has continued to advance, even employing radio astronomy satellites to create interferometers with baselines considerably greater than the Earth's

High-energy astronomy includes X-ray astronomy,Gamma-Ray astronomy,and Extreme UV astronomy.High energy astronomy is the study of astronomical objects that release electromagnetic radiation of highly energetic wavelengths.

Occultation astronomy is the observation of one celestial object occults or eclipses another .An occultation is a term used in astronomy to describe when one object is obscured by another object passing between it and the observer.Asteroid occultation observations measure the asteroid's profile to the kilometer level.

Cosmic ray astronomy The goal of cosmic ray astronomy is to find and investigate the sources of extremely high-energy cosmic rays. It is one of a kind in that it uses charged particles as information carriers.

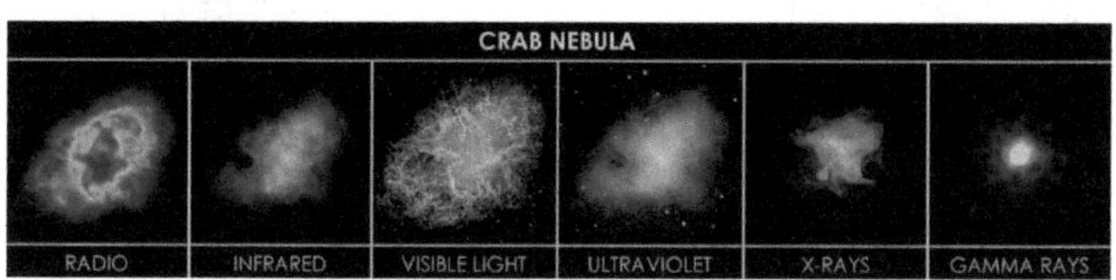

The Crab Nebula as seen in various wavelengths

Optical Astronomy

Almost all observational astronomy was done in the visual spectrum with optical telescopes for much of its history. Visible-light astronomy is part of optical astronomy which differs from astronomies based on invisible types of light in the electromagnetic radiation spectrum, such as radio waves, infrared waves, ultraviolet waves, X-ray waves and gamma-ray waves. Visible light ranges from 380 to 750 nanometers in wavelength.

Astronomy was limited to unassisted vision before the invention of telescopes. As evidenced by the naming of several constellations, humans have been staring at stars and other objects in the night sky for thousands of years.

Hans Lippershey, a German-Dutch spectacle maker, is widely acknowledged as the inventor of the optical telescope. Lippershey is the first individual to file a patent application for a telescope although Galileo played a large role in the development and creation of telescopes. On 25 August 1609, Galileo demonstrated one of his early telescopes, with a magnification of up to 8 or 9.

The telescope is the most important instrument in all modern observational astronomy. This accomplishes two goals: it gathers more light so that faint objects can be seen, and it magnifies the image so that small and distant objects can be seen. Optical astronomy necessitates telescopes with extremely precise optical components. Large telescopes are housed in domes, both to protect them from the weather and to stabilize the environmental conditions.

The best place for an optical telescope for observation purposes is unquestionably in space. The telescope can observe without being influenced by the atmosphere there. Lifting telescopes into orbit, however, is still expensive. As a result, certain mountain peaks with a large proportion of clear days and usually good atmospheric conditions with good seeing conditions are the next best options used.

In today's world, space telescopes, which are located outside of the Earth's atmosphere, are used to acquire the finest quality images and data. This enables for far clearer views since the atmosphere does not interfere with the image and viewing quality of the telescope, allowing for much better detail and the study of far more distant or low-light objects. This also means that observations can be done at any time of day, rather not only during the night.

The Hubble Space Telescope is a NASA-built space telescope that was launched into low-Earth orbit in 1990. The Hubble Space Telescope's four primary instruments look for objects in the near ultraviolet, visible, and near infrared spectral ranges. Hubble's photos are among the most comprehensive ever obtained, resulting to numerous astrophysics achievements, including the precise determination of the universe's expansion rate.

The James Webb Space Telescope is the formal successor of the Hubble Space Telescope. It will enable a broad range of investigations across the fields of astronomy and cosmology, including observations of some of the most distant events and objects in the Universe, such as the formation of the first galaxies, and detailed atmospheric characterization of potentially habitable exo planets, as well as observations of some of the most distant events and objects in the Universe, such as the formation of the first galaxies.

In visible-light astronomy, there are three basic types of telescopes.

Refracting telescopes, which use lenses to form the image.

Due to its inexpensive cost and ease of use, amateur astronomers frequently use it to observe brighter objects such as the Moon and planets. A refracting telescope, also known as a refractor, is an optical telescope that forms an image using a lens as its objective. It is also known as a dioptric telescope.

The use of refracting telescopes in astronomy and for terrestrial viewing was well-known. Singlet refractors were used in many early solar system discoveries. Refracting telescopic lenses are widely employed in photography, and they are also used in Earth orbit.

The earliest optical telescopes were refractors. The first record of a refracting telescope came in the Netherlands in 1608, when Hans Lippershey, a spectacle manufacturer from Middelburg, failed to patent one.Galileo Galilei, who happened to be in Venice in May 1609, learned about the invention, built his own version, and used it to make astronomical discoveries.

Galileo's discovery of Jupiter's four largest moons in 1609 was one of the most well-known uses of the refracting telescope. Furthermore, several decades later, early refractors were used to discover Titan, Saturn's largest moon, as well as three other moons of Saturn.

All refracting telescopes use the same principles. The combination of an objective lens and some type of eyepiece is used to gather more light than the human eye is able to collect on its own, focus it , and present the viewer with a brighter, clearer, and magnified virtual image.

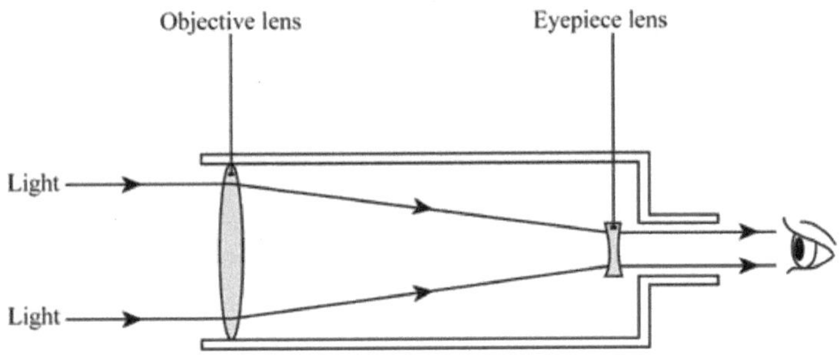

Refracting telescope principle

Refracting telescopes were employed for pioneering work on astrophotography and spectroscopy in the nineteenth century, and the related device, the heliometer, was used for the first time to determine the distance to another star.

Their tiny apertures did not lead to as many discoveries, and many astronomical objects were simply not visible until the advent of long-exposure photography, by which time the renown and peculiarities of reflecting telescopes had begun to surpass those of refractors.Some other discoveries include the Moons of Mars, a fifth Moon of Jupiter, and many double star discoveries including Sirius (the Dog star). Refactors were often used for positional astronomy.

Reflecting telescopes, which use mirrors to form the image.

Commonly used for scientific purposes. Isaac Newton designed the reflecting telescope in the 17th century as a replacement for the refracting telescope, which suffered from severe chromatic aberration at the time. Reflecting telescopes cause additional sorts of optical distortions, although they have the advantage of allowing very large diameter objectives.

A reflecting telescope (also known as a reflector) is a type of telescope that employs a single or many curved mirrors to reflect light and create a picture. Reflectors make up nearly all of the large telescopes used in astronomy research. Extra optical components may be used to increase image quality or to put the image in a mechanically advantageous position in reflecting telescopes. Reflecting telescopes are sometimes referred to as catoptric telescopes since they use mirrors.

Reflecting telescopes have become quite popular in astronomy, with several well-known telescopes, such as the Hubble Space Telescope, as well as popular amateur ones, employing this design. In addition, the reflection telescope technique has been adapted to other electromagnetic wavelengths; for example, image-forming optics in X-ray telescopes are made using the reflection principle.

The basic optical element of a reflector telescope that forms an image at the focal plane is a curved primary mirror. The focal length is the distance between the mirror and the focal plane. A secondary mirror may be added to modify the optical characteristics and/or redirect the light to film, digital sensors, or an eyepiece for visual observation.

Film or a digital sensor may be located here to record the image, or a secondary mirror may be added to modify the optical characteristics and/or redirect the light to film, digital sensors, or an eyepiece for visual observation.

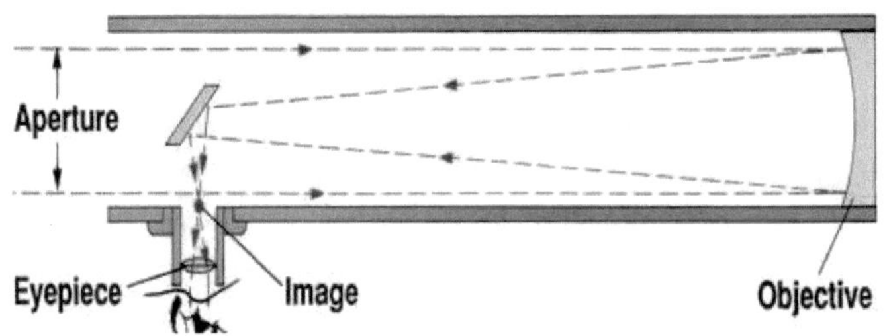

Reflecting telescopes principle

Reflectors make up the majority of big research-grade astronomical telescopes. Because certain wavelengths are absorbed when travelling through glass elements like those found in a refractor or a catadioptric telescope, reflectors work in a wider range of light.

Catadioptric telescopes which use a combination of lenses and mirrors to form the image; essentially a combination of refracting and reflecting telescopes.

A catadioptric optical system combines refraction and reflection in a single optical system, typically using dioptric lenses and curved mirrors (catoptrics).Catadioptric telescopes are optical telescopes that produce an image by combining specially curved mirrors and lenses. This is typically done so that the telescope has a higher overall degree of error correction than all-lens or all-mirror counterparts, resulting in a broader aberration-free field of view.

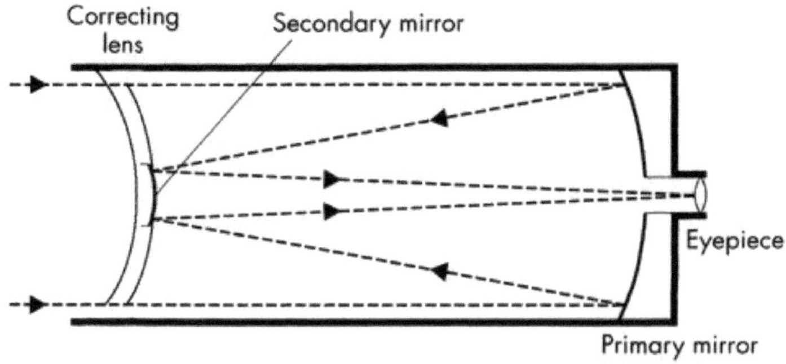

Catadioptric telescopes principle

Catadioptric telescopes are optical telescopes that produce an image by combining specially curved mirrors and lenses. This is typically done so that the telescope has a higher overall degree of error correction than all-lens or all-mirror counterparts, resulting in a broader aberration-free field of view. They can use basic all-spherical surfaces and a folded optical path to reduce the mass of the telescope, making it easier to produce.

Infrared astronomy

Infrared astronomy began in the 1830s, a few decades after the discovery of infrared light by William Herschel in 1800. Infrared astronomy is a branch of astronomy that focuses on using infrared (IR) radiation to observe and analyze celestial objects.Infrared light has a wavelength of 0.75 to

300 micro metres, which is halfway between visible radiation (380 to 750 nanometers) and sub millimeter waves.

Early progress was slow, and definitive detections of astronomical objects other than the Sun and Moon in infrared light did not occur until the early twentieth century. Attempts to detect infrared radiation from other celestial sources began in the 1830s and continued throughout the 19th century. During an expedition to Tenerife in 1856 to test his ideas about mountain top astronomy, Charles Piazzi Smyth, the Astronomer Royal for Scotland, discovered radiation from the Moon for the first time.

Infrared astronomy progressed slowly in the early twentieth century, with the development of thermopile detectors capable of accurate infrared photometry and sensitive to a few hundreds of stars by Seth Barnes Nicholson and Edison Pettit.

Because the same mirrors or lenses are usually effective over a wavelength range that encompasses both visible and infrared light, infrared and optical astronomy are frequently done using the same telescopes. Solid state detectors are employed in both disciplines, albeit the types of solid state photodetectors used are different.

Near-infrared radiation, defined as infrared radiation with wavelengths just longer than visible light, behaves similarly to visible light and may be detected using similar solid-state equipment. As a result, many quasars, stars, and galaxies have been discovered. The near infrared section of the spectrum, along with the near ultraviolet, is frequently included in the "optical" spectrum. Many optical telescopes, such as those at Keck Observatory, are capable of operating in both the near infrared and visible wavelengths.

Galaxy through Visible and Infrared spectrum

The 2MASS and WISE astronomy surveys' infrared readings have been particularly successful in revealing previously unknown star clusters. Infrared telescopes, which include most major optical telescopes and a few specialized infrared telescopes, require liquid nitrogen cooling and protection from warm objects. Because objects with temperatures of a few hundred kelvins emit the majority of their thermal energy at infrared wavelengths.

The Earth's atmosphere is the primary limiting factor for infrared sensitivity from ground-based telescopes. Water vapor absorbs a lot of infrared radiation, while the atmosphere emits infrared wavelengths as well. As a result, most infrared telescopes are constructed in very dry locations at high altitudes, above the majority of the water vapor in the atmosphere.Infrared observatories have also been launched into space, such as the Spitzer Space Telescope, Herschel Space Observatory, and, most recently, the James Webb Space Telescope.

Space, like visible light telescopes, is an appropriate location for infrared telescopes. Space telescopes can reach higher resolution because they are free of blurring created by the Earth's atmosphere, as well as infrared absorption induced by the atmosphere. Infrared astronomy has unique needs, such as very low dark currents to enable for extended integration times, low noise readout circuits, and sometimes very high pixel counts.

Because objects with temperatures of a few hundred kelvins emit the majority of their thermal energy at infrared wavelengths, this is the case. If infrared detectors were not maintained cold, the detector's own radiation would generate noise that would exceed that of any celestial source. This is especially true in the spectrum's mid-infrared and far-infrared portions.

Many space telescopes detect electromagnetic radiation in a wavelength range that overlaps with the infrared wavelength range at least to some extent. Only a few of the sensors on numerous space telescopes can observe infrared light.

Some of the most significant space observatories and instruments are listed below:

- Cosmic Background Explorer (COBE) satellite (1989-1993) Diffuse Infrared Background Experiment (DIRBE) instrument
- Hubblespace telescope (1990-) Near Infrared Camera and Multi-ObjectSpectrometer (NICMOS) instrument (1997-1999, 2002-2008)
- Hubble space telescope (1990-) Wide Field Camera 3 (WFC3) camera (2009-) observes infrared.

The other discipline of astronomy and astrophysics that deals with objects visible in far-infrared radiation (wavelengths ranging from 30 m to submillimeter wavelengths approximately 450 m) is known as far-infrared astronomy.Stars aren't particularly brilliant in the far-infrared, but emission from very cold matter (140 Kelvin or less) can be seen, which isn't visible at shorter wavelengths. This is caused due to interstellar dust in molecular clouds emitting heat radiation.

Because the Earth's atmosphere is opaque in most of the far-infrared, satellites like the Herschel Space Observatory, Spitzer Space Telescope, IRAS, and Infrared Space Observatory do the majority of far-infrared astronomy.The 2MASS and WISE astronomy surveys' infrared readings have been particularly successful in revealing previously unknown star clusters.

Radio astronomy

In 1933, Karl Jansky of Bell Telephone Laboratories claimed the first detection of radio waves from an astronomical object when he observed radiation from the Milky Way. Following observations, a variety of possible sources of radio emission have been found. Stars and galaxies are among them, as are totally new types of phenomena like radio galaxies, quasars, pulsars, and masers. Radio astronomy was used to discover the cosmic microwave background radiation, which is used as support for the Big Bang idea.

Physicists believed that radio waves could be seen from cosmic sources before Jansky discovered the radiation from Milky Way in the 1930s. The equations of James Clerk Maxwell, published in the 1860s, demonstrated that electromagnetic radiation is related to electricity and magnetism, and that it can exist at any wavelength. An experiment by German astrophysicists Johannes Wilsing and Julius Scheiner in 1896 and a centimetre wave radiation apparatus built by Oliver Lodge between 1897 and 1900 were among the attempts to detect radio emission from the Sun.

In April 1933, Jansky presented his discovery, and the field of radio astronomy was founded. In 1937, Grote Reber was inspired by Jansky's work and built a 9-meter-diameter parabolic radio telescope in his backyard. He began by duplicating Jansky's observations before doing the first radio frequency sky survey. James Stanley Hey, a British Army research officer, made the first observation of radio waves generated by the Sun on February 27, 1942. Later that year, like Jansky, George Clark Southworth of Bell Labs observed radiowaves from the sun.

Radio astronomers observe objects in the radio spectrum using a variety of techniques. To investigate the emission of an intense radio source, instruments can simply be pointed towards it. Multiple overlapping scans can be recorded and stitched together in a mosaic image to "image" a part of the sky in greater detail. The sort of instrument used is determined by the signal's strength and the level of information required.Radio astronomy is carried out with the use of enormous radio antennas known as radio telescopes, which can be used alone or in conjunction with other telescopes using techniques like radio interferometry and aperture synthesis.

Radio astronomy can attain great angular resolution using interferometry because the resolving power of an interferometer is determined by the distance between its components rather than the size of its components.

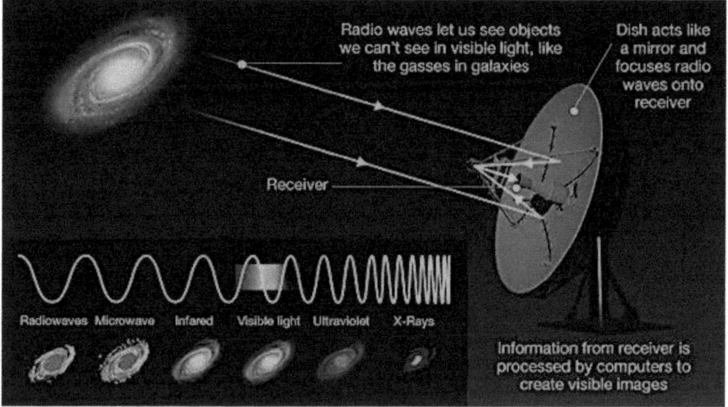

Radio Astronomy telescopes

To receive transmissions with a low signal-to-noise ratio, radio telescopes may need to be incredibly huge. Radio telescopes must also be significantly larger than optical counterparts because angular resolution is a function of the diameter of the "objective" in proportion to the wavelength of the electromagnetic radiation being seen.

Radio interferometry was invented in 1946 by British radio astronomer Martin Ryle and Australian engineers, radio physicists, and radio astronomers Joseph Lade Pawsey and Ruby Payne-Scott in response to the challenge of reaching high resolutions with single radio telescopes. Modern radio interferometers are made up of many radio telescopes that are connected by coaxial cable, waveguide, optical fibre, or another type of transmission line to observe the same object. This not only enhances the total signal gathered, but it can also be employed in an aperture synthesis process to greatly improve resolution.

This technique works by superimposing ("interfering") the signal waves from the various telescopes, based on the premise that waves with the same phase add to each other, while waves with opposite phases cancel out. This results in a combined telescope the size of the array's farthest apart antennas.

A large number of different separations between different telescopes are required to produce a high quality image (the projected separation between any two telescopes as seen from the radio source is referred to as a "baseline") – as many different baselines as possible are required to obtain a good quality image. The Very Large Array, for example, includes 27 telescopes that provide 351 independent baselines at the same time.

Improvements in radio telescope receiver stability began in the 1970s, allowing telescopes from all over the world and even in Earth orbit to be coupled to perform very-long-baseline interferometry. Data received at each antenna is matched with time information, usually from a nearby atomic clock, and then saved for subsequent analysis on magnetic tape or hard drive, rather than physically connecting the antennas.

The data is eventually correlated with data from other antennas that were similarly recorded to form the final image. It is conceivable to create an antenna that is effectively the size of the Earth using this technology. The huge distances between the telescopes allow for extremely high angular resolutions, far larger than in any other branch of astronomy.

The Very Long Baseline Array (with telescopes spanning North America) and the European VLBI Network are the two most important VLBI arrays in operation today (telescopes in Europe, China, South Africa and Puerto

Rico). Normally, each array works alone, however on rare occasions, projects are seen working together to boost sensitivity. Global VLBI is the term for this. There are further VLBI networks named the LBA (Long Baseline Array) that operate in Australia and New Zealand, as well as arrays in Japan, China, and South Korea that observe together to form the East-Asian VLBI Network (EAVN).

Radio telescopes were also used to detect the cosmic microwave background radiation for the first time. Radio telescopes, on the other hand, have been used to study objects considerably closer to home, such as views of the Sun and solar activity, as well as radar mapping of the planets.

The discovery of various kinds of new objects, such as pulsars, quasars, and radio galaxies, has resulted in significant advances in astronomical understanding ,thanks to radio astronomy. This is due to the fact that radio astronomy allows us to observe things that optical astronomy cannot.

High-energy astronomy

High-energy astronomy is the study of celestial objects that emit highly intense electromagnetic radiation. X-ray astronomy, gamma-ray astronomy, and extreme UV astronomy, as well as neutrinos and cosmic ray investigations, are all part of it. Black holes, neutron stars, active galactic nuclei, supernovae, kilonovae, supernova remnants, and gamma ray bursts are some of the astronomical objects examined in this discipline.

The study of the processes that occur within stars, black holes, and supernovae is known as high-energy astrophysics. The high-energy electromagnetic radiation and particles that these processes release, such as x-rays, ultraviolet light, and gamma rays, can be measured and monitored. Computer simulations are used to supplement these observations.

X-ray astronomy

X-ray astronomy is an astronomical observational branch concerned with the study of X-ray emitted from astronomical objects. Astronomical objects with extremely hot gases with temperatures ranging from a million kelvin (K) to hundreds of millions of kelvin are projected to emit X-rays (MK).

X-ray astronomy makes use of a special form of space telescope that can observe x-ray radiation that optical telescopes cannot.Although theory anticipated that the Sun and stars would be prominent X-ray producers, there was no way to confirm this because most alien X-rays are blocked by Earth's atmosphere.

V-2s converted to sounding rockets revealed the existence of solar X-rays in the mid-twentieth century, and the detection of extra terrestrial X-rays has been the primary or secondary mission of many satellites since 1958. A sounding rocket detected the first cosmic beyond the Solar System X-ray source in 1962. The X-ray emission of Scorpius X-1 (Sco X-1) ,the first X-ray source discovered in the constellation Scorpius is 10,000 times more than its visible emission, but the Sun's is around a million times less. Many thousands of X-ray sources have since been discovered.

The hot ionised medium (HIM), which consists of a coronal cloud ejection from star surfaces at 106-107 K and generates X-rays, is of interest. Satellites that research X-ray emissions from astronomical objects are known as X-ray astronomy satellites. As part of a discipline of space science, satellites that can detect and send data regarding X-ray emissions are deployed. Because X-rays are absorbed by the Earth's atmosphere, X-ray detection instruments must be carried to high altitudes by balloons, sounding rockets, and satellites.

The Sun was observed with the first X-ray telescope in astronomy. In 1963, a rocket-borne telescope took the first X-ray picture of the Sun using a grazing incidence telescope. X-ray astronomy detectors have been constructed and configured largely for energy detection, with some wavelength detection thrown in for good measure, utilising a range of techniques that are usually limited to the technology available at the time.

Individual X-rays (photons of X-ray electromagnetic radiation) are collected by X-ray detectors, which count the number of photons collected (intensity), the energy (0.12 to 120 keV) of the photons collected, wavelength or the rate at which the photons are detected (counts per hour) to provide information about the object that is emitting them.

An X-ray telescope (XRT) is a telescope that uses the X-ray spectrum to observe distant objects. X-ray telescopes must be mounted on high altitude rockets, balloons, or artificial satellites to rise above the Earth's atmosphere, which is opaque to X-rays.

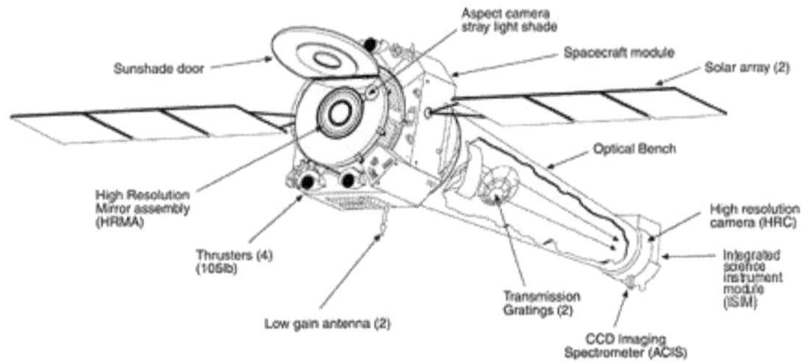

X-ray telescope principle

The optics focusing or collimating that collects the radiation entering the telescope and the detector on which the radiation is collected and measured are the two essential elements of the telescope. These have been made using a range of various designs and technology.

From galaxy clusters to black holes in active galactic nuclei (AGN) to galactic objects like supernova remnants, stars, and binary stars containing a white dwarf -cataclysmic variable stars and super soft X-ray sources, neutron star, or black hole, a variety of astrophysical objects emit, fluoresce, or reflect X-rays (X-ray binaries).

The Moon is the most visible X-ray emitter in the Solar System, yet most of its X-ray brightness comes from reflected solar X-rays.

Striking to comprehend the apparent source's emission of X-rays aids in understanding the Sun, the cosmos as a whole, and how these effect us on Earth, much as it does with sources already successfully modelled by X-ray astrophysics.

An astronomical model addressing the likely source of X-ray emission can be created using the observed X-ray spectrum and spectral emission results for other wavelength ranges.

The Chandra X-Ray Observatory is among the recent satellite observatories launched by NASA, and by the Space Agencies of Europe, Japan, and Russia.

The Einstein Observatory (1978–1981), also known as HEAO-2, was the first orbiting X-ray observatory with a Wolter Type I telescope.It obtained high-resolution X-ray images in the energy range from 0.1 to 4 keV of stars of all types, supernova remnants, galaxies, and clusters of galaxies.

Theoretical X-ray astronomy is also a field of theoretical astronomy that studies the theoretical astrophysics and astrochemistry of X-ray creation, emission, and detection in celestial objects.

Theoretical X-ray astronomy, like theoretical astrophysics, employs a variety of methods and techniques that includes

- Analytical models to approximate the behaviour of a potential X-ray source and
- Computational numerical simulations to mimic observational data.

Once possible observational repercussions have been identified, they can be compared to experimental findings. Observers can look for data that contradicts a model or aids in the selection of one model over another.

The majority of the topics examined by theoreticians in astrophysics, astrochemistry, astrometry, and other aspects of astronomy involve X-rays and X-ray sources.

Gamma-ray astronomy

The study of gamma rays from astronomical objects, the most powerful form of electromagnetic radiation, with photon energy exceeding 100 keV, is known as gamma-ray astronomy. The mechanisms that emit gamma rays are diverse, mostly identical to those that emit X-rays but at higher energies, such as electron–positron annihilation, and gamma decay in space-reflecting extreme events such as supernovae and hypernovae, and the behaviour of matter under extreme conditions, such as pulsars and blazars.

In the 1960s, it became feasible to observe gamma rays for the first time. Because gamma-rays are very infrequent, even a "bright" source requires several minutes of observation time before it is even discovered, and because gamma-rays are difficult to focus, resulting in very low resolution, their observation is far more challenging than that of X-rays or visible light.

Non-gamma-ray backgrounds limit gamma-ray astronomy observations at lower energies, and the quantity of photons that can be detected at higher energies. For advancement in the field, larger area detectors and improved background suppression are required.

Because most gamma rays from space are absorbed by the Earth's atmosphere, gamma-ray astronomy could not advance until balloons and spacecraft could place detectors above all or most of the atmosphere.In 1961, the Explorer 11 satellite carried the first gamma-ray telescope into orbit, which detected less than 100 cosmic gamma-ray photons. They appeared to be coming from every direction in the Universe, assuming a homogeneous "gamma-ray backdrop."

The interaction of cosmic rays very powerful charged particles in space with interstellar gas would provide such a background.

Solar flares were the first true astrophysical gamma-ray sources. Solar flares on August 4 and 7, 1972, and November 22, 1977, both produced nuclear gamma rays. A solar flare is an explosion in the Sun's atmosphere that was first observed visually.

Solar flares emit tremendous volumes of radiation spanning the whole electromagnetic spectrum, from radio waves to high-energy gamma rays. These gamma rays can be seen, allowing scientists to figure out the principal outcomes of the energy produced, which isn't possible with other wavelengths.

The OSO 3 satellite's detector first identified significant gamma-ray emission from our galaxy in 1967. It discovered 621 cosmic gamma ray-related occurrences. The SAS-2 (1972) and Cos-B (1975–1982) satellites, on the other hand, made significant advances in the field of gamma-ray astronomy. These two satellites gave a fascinating look into the high-energy universe also known as the 'violent' universe since gamma rays are produced by high-speed collisions and comparable activities in space.

Two massive gamma-ray bubbles, spanning roughly 25,000 light-years across, were discovered near the core of the Milky Way in November 2010 using the Fermi Gamma-ray Space Telescope. These high-energy radiation bubbles are thought to be the result of a large black hole emerging or evidence of a massive star formation burst millions of years ago. After filtering out the "fog of background gamma-rays suffusing the sky," scientists spotted them. This discovery backed with prior evidence that the Milky Way's centre contains a massive, unidentified "structure."

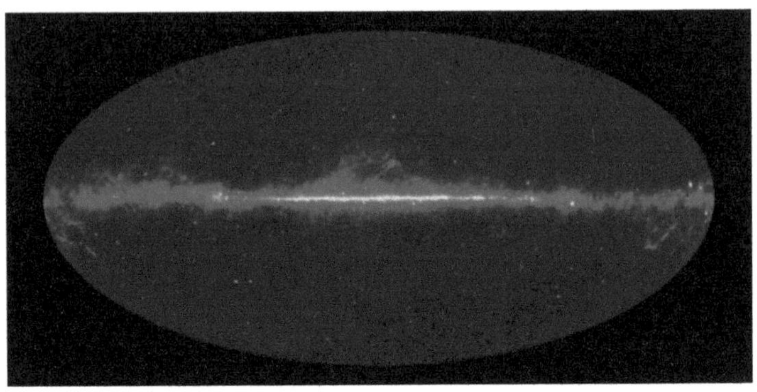

Fermi Gamma Ray Telescope: Studying the High-Energy Cosmos

The most powerful gamma ray sources are also the most powerful sources of any sort of electromagnetic radiation currently known. They are astronomical "long duration burst" sources of gamma rays "long" in this case referring to a few tens of seconds, and they are extremely rare. During the collision of two neutron stars, or a neutron star and a black hole, "short" gamma-ray bursts of two seconds or less, which are not connected with supernovae, are thought to emit gamma rays.

When a gamma-ray burst (GRB) is discovered by many satellites, the gamma-ray burst coordinates network (GCN) communicates information regarding its location, termed notices. The GCN also receives and distributes circulars, which are notifications concerning follow-up observations, to persons and institutions who are interested. Ground-based and space-based optical, radio, and X-ray observatories may conduct follow-up observations.

HAWC, MAGIC, HESS, and VERITAS are examples of ground-based gamma-ray observatories. Because their effective regions can be many orders of magnitude bigger than a satellite, ground-based observatories can probe a wider energy range than space-based observatories.

The Fermi team published its second catalogue of gamma-ray sources discovered by the satellite's Large Area Telescope (LAT) in 2011, which included 1,873 objects emitting the highest-energy kind of light. Blazars account for 57% of the sources. Over half of the sources are active galaxies, with gamma-ray radiation produced by their central black holes.

Ultraviolet astronomy

UV astronomy is the study of celestial objects' ultraviolet spectra. Ultraviolet light originates in a hotter part of the electromagnetic spectrum than visible light. In the ultraviolet, for example, interstellar gas with temperatures close to 1,000,000 kelvins is extremely visible. It has revealed a wealth of information on the Sun's chemical abundances and activities, as well as those of other stellar objects like white dwarfs.Ultraviolet astronomy is the study of electromagnetic radiation with wavelengths between 10 and 320 nanometres. Because the Earth's atmosphere absorbs the majority of light at these wavelengths, observations at these wavelengths must be made from the high atmosphere or from space.

The introduction of rockets capable of lifting instruments above Earth's atmosphere, which absorbs most electromagnetic radiation of ultraviolet wavelengths (approximately 100 to 4,000 angstroms) from celestial sources, made UV astronomy possible. Even at the highest altitudes that balloons may reach, a significant amount of radiation is lost. Attempts to picture the Sun's ultraviolet spectrum from balloons failed in the 1920s, and it wasn't until 1946 that a rocket-borne camera succeeded.

Since the early 1960s, the United States and a number of other countries have launched unmanned satellite observatories carrying telescopes with specific coatings for high UV reflectivity into Earth orbit. The US National Aeronautics and Space Administration (NASA) launched eight Orbiting Solar Observatories between 1962 and 1975, allowing astronomers to gather millions of ultraviolet spectra of the Sun's corona. From 1968 through 1981, a series of US spacecraft known as Orbiting Astronomical Observatories allowed researchers to examine the interstellar medium and distant stars in the spectral range of 1,200 to 4,000 angstroms.

UV telescopes have tremendously improved our understanding of the stars in astronomy. Temperature spikes in the outer atmospheres of stars such as the sun are well known, but the mechanisms of this temperature rise are poorly understood.

UV telescopes give a plethora of information about celestial objects' hot and energetic processes. This is because the more energy an object radiates at short wavelengths, the hotter it is. Because UV radiation has shorter wavelengths than visible light, heated objects seem brighter in the UV.

Galaxy through Visible and Ultraviolet spectrum

Ultraviolet radiation is emitted by hotter things throughout their early and late stages of development. Most stars would decline in prominence in the Earth's sky when viewed in UV light. Some very young massive stars and some very old massive stars and galaxies might be visible when they grew hotter and produced higher-energy radiation approaching their birth or death. Many directions along the Milky Way would be obscured by clouds of gas and dust.

The centre of galaxies is another region where hot, high-energy conditions exist. At the heart of the so-called active galaxies are powerful high-energy sources. Huge jets of hot, high-energy material frequently emerge from these galaxies. An huge black hole at the galactic centre is thought to be the source of the extreme energy output.

As a result, a lot of UV astronomy is focused on energetic processes in stars and galaxies. The ultraviolet telescope, for example, can see hot parts of star atmospheres that are invisible to optical telescopes yet give a wealth of information.

Ultraviolet telescopes are particularly interested in the crowded, turbulent areas at the centres of several galaxies.Although additional UV instruments have flown on smaller observatories such as GALEX, sounding rockets, and the Space Shuttle, the Hubble Space Telescope and FUSE are the most recent big space telescopes that view the near and far UV spectrum of the sky.

Cosmic Ray astronomy

High-energy protons and atomic nuclei known as cosmic rays travel through space at almost the speed of light. They come from the Sun, outside the Solar System in our own galaxy, and from faraway galaxies. Cosmic rays collide with Earth's atmosphere, releasing showers of secondary particles, some of which reach the surface but the majority of which are redirected into space by the magnetosphere or heliosphere.

About 99 percent of primary cosmic rays, which originate outside the Earth's atmosphere, are bare nuclei of well-known atoms stripped of their electron shells, while about 1% are solitary electrons a sort of beta particle. About 90% of the nuclei are simple protons, such as hydrogen nuclei; 9% are alpha particles, which are identical to helium nuclei; and 1% are heavier element nuclei, known as HZE ions. These proportions fluctuate dramatically across the energy spectrum of cosmic rays. Only a small percentage are stable antimatter particles like positrons or antiprotons.

The exact nature of the remaining portion is still being researched. Anti-alpha particles have not been found despite an intense search from Earth orbit.

A 1934 proposal by Baade and Zwicky that cosmic rays originated from supernovae was one of the first attempts to explain their origins. Horace W. Babcock proposed in 1948 that magnetic variable stars could be a source of cosmic rays. Sekido et al. (1951) later recognised the Crab Nebula as a cosmic ray source. Since then, a slew of new cosmic ray sources have emerged, including supernovae, active galactic nuclei, quasars, and gamma-ray bursts.

The two types of cosmic rays are High-energy particles emitted by the sun, mainly in solar eruptions, are known as galactic cosmic rays (GCR) and extragalactic cosmic rays (EGCR).However, the phrase "cosmic ray" is frequently applied to the extrasolar flux alone.

Protons and alpha particles make up 99 percent of primary cosmic rays, with a little number of heavier nuclei (1 percent) and an extremely small proportion of positrons and antiprotons. Photons, leptons, and hadrons, such as electrons, positrons, muons, and pions, are secondary cosmic rays produced by the decay of primary cosmic rays as they contact an atmosphere. The last three of these were discovered in cosmic rays for the first time.

Primary cosmic rays come from beyond the Solar System, and occasionally even the Milky Way. They are transformed to secondary particles when they encounter with the Earth's atmosphere. The 28 percent mass ratio of helium to hydrogen nuclei is similar to the 24 percent primordial elemental abundance ratio of these elements. The additional heavier nuclei that are typical nucleosynthesis end products, namely lithium, beryllium, and boron, make up the remaining fraction.

HZE ions are cosmic rays made up of charged nuclei heavier than helium. HZE ions, despite their scarcity, contribute significantly to an astronaut's radiation dosage in space due to their high charge and heavy nature.

In primary cosmic rays, satellite experiments discovered positrons and a few antiprotons, accounting for fewer than 1% of the particles in primary cosmic rays. Large amounts of antimatter from the Big Bang, or even complex antimatter throughout the universe, do not appear to be the source of these. Rather, they appear to be formed up entirely of these two fundamental particles, which were created by energetic processes.

Secondary cosmic rays -Cosmic rays clash with atoms and molecules in the Earth's atmosphere, primarily oxygen and nitrogen, to produce secondary cosmic rays. The impact creates a cascade of lighter particles that rain down, including x-rays, protons, alpha particles, pions, muons, electrons, neutrinos, and neutrons, known as air shower secondary radiation. All of the secondary particles created by the collision continue on routes that are within one degree of the original path of the parent particle.

Neutrons and charged mesons such as positive or negative pions and kaons are common products of such collisions. Some of them eventually decay into muons and neutrinos, which can reach the Earth's surface. Some high-energy muons can even penetrate shallow mines for a short distance, and most neutrinos pass through the Earth without interacting with anything else. Others decompose into photons, resulting in electromagnetic cascades. As a result, electrons and positrons usually outnumber photons in air showers.

Many particle detectors, including cloud chambers, bubble chambers, water-Cherenkov, and scintillation detectors, can easily detect these particles, as well as muons.There are two types of detecting techniques. First, balloon-borne equipment may directly detect primary cosmic rays in space or at high altitude. Second, the identification of secondary particles via indirect means, such as large air showers at higher energy.

While there have been plans and prototypes for air shower detection from space and balloons, the present investigations for high-energy cosmic rays are on the ground. Direct detection is, on average, more accurate than indirect detection. However, the flux of cosmic rays diminishes with increasing energy, making direct detection difficult over 1 PeV. Several techniques are used to achieve both direct and indirect detection.

Cosmic rays from the Milky Way are one of the most significant obstacles to crewed spacecraft interplanetary travel. Electronics on outgoing probes are likewise vulnerable to cosmic rays. A single flipped bit, perhaps triggered by a cosmic ray, was blamed for a failure aboard the Voyager 2 space probe in 2010. To reduce the damage caused by cosmic rays to electronics and humans, strategies such as physical or magnetic shielding for spacecraft have been suggested.

Based on the quantity of energetic particle radiation recorded by the RAD on the Mars Science Laboratory while travelling from Earth to Mars in 2011–2012, NASA scientists revealed on May 31, 2013, that a possible crewed trip to Mars may pose a bigger radiation risk than previously thought.

Comparison of radiation exposures, including the quantity detected by the RAD on the MSL during its journey from Earth to Mars (2011–2013),passengers and workers on jet airliners are exposed to at least 10 times the cosmic ray dose that individuals at sea level experience when flying at a height of 12 kilometres (39,000 feet). Polar routes near the geomagnetic poles are particularly dangerous for aircraft.

Edward P. Ney proposed a function for cosmic rays in climate in 1959, and Robert E. Dickinson proposed it in 1975. Cosmic rays have been suggested as a possible cause of major climatic change and mass extinction in the past. According to Adrian Mellott and Mikhail Medvedev, the motion of the Earth relative to the galactic plane and increases in cosmic ray exposure cause 62-million-year cycles in biological marine populations.

The researchers believe that this, as well as gamma ray bombardments from nearby supernovae, may have influenced cancer and mutation rates, as well as being linked to significant changes in the Earth's temperature and the Ordovician mass extinctions.

Henrik Svensmark, a controversial Danish physicist, has proposed that because solar variation influences cosmic ray flux on Earth, it affects the rate of cloud formation and so is an indirect cause of global warming.

According to a few researchers, a nearby supernova or series of supernovas triggered the extinction of the Pliocene marine megafauna by significantly boosting radiation levels to dangerous levels for large seafaring creatures.

Neutrino astronomy

Neutrino astronomy is a discipline of astronomy that uses neutrino detectors in special observatories to examine celestial objects. Neutrinos are produced by some types of radioactive decay, nuclear reactions such as those seen in the Sun or high-energy astrophysical phenomena, nuclear reactors, and when cosmic rays collide with atoms in the atmosphere.

In contrast to photons, neutrinos rarely interact with matter, therefore they are unlikely to scatter along their path. As a result, neutrinos provide a once-in-a-lifetime opportunity to view processes that are otherwise inaccessible to optical observatories, such as reactions in the Sun's core. In comparison to charged particle cosmic rays, neutrinos have a very strong pointing orientation.

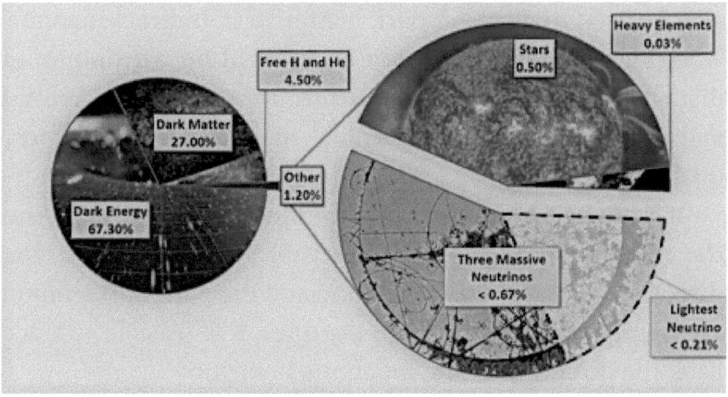

Neutrinos in universe

Neutrino detectors must have high target masses, often millions of tonnes, since neutrinos interact weakly. To eliminate background signal, the detectors must additionally use shielding and effective software.

Only the surface of celestial entities, such as the Sun, can be directly visible while studying them with light. Any light produced in a star's core will interact with gas particles in the star's outer layers, requiring hundreds of thousands of years to reach the surface, making direct observation of the core impossible. Because neutrinos are produced in the cores of stars as a result of stellar fusion, neutrino astronomy can be used to study the core.

Other neutrinos sources, like as neutrinos emitted by supernovae, have been discovered. The Supernova Early Warning System (SNEWS) is a collaboration of several neutrino experiments that looks for an increase in neutrino flux that could indicate a supernova.

Detecting neutrinos from other sources, including as active galactic nuclei (AGN), gamma-ray bursts, and starburst galaxies, is now a goal. Neutrino astronomy may also be used to discover dark matter in an indirect manner.

A high angular resolution is essential for astronomy of distant objects. Because neutrinos are electrically neutral and interact weakly, they travel in straight lines almost unaffected.

If a neutrino interacts with a muon within a detector, the muon produces an observable trail. Because the direction of the arriving neutrino and the path of the muon are tightly associated at high energies, it is feasible to trace back the direction of the incoming neutrino.

The main or secondary cosmic rays produced by powerful astrophysical processes produce these high-energy neutrinos. Observing neutrinos could reveal information about these processes that isn't available through electromagnetic radiation.

Multi-wavelength astronomy was utilised to prove spatial synchronicity in the case of a neutrino observed from a distant blazar, confirming the blazar as the source. Neutrinos may be utilised to enhance electromagnetic and gravitational measurements in the future, resulting in multi-messenger astronomy.

Gravitational wave astronomy

Gravitational-wave astronomy is a new branch of observational astronomy that aims to collect observational data about objects like neutron stars and black holes, events like supernovae, and processes like those of the early universe shortly after the Big Bang using gravitational waves -minor distortions of spacetime predicted by Albert Einstein's theory of general relativity.

The theory of relativity provides a solid theoretical foundation for gravitational waves. Although they are a specific consequence of general relativity, they are a common property of all theories of gravity that obey special relativity. They were initially predicted by Einstein in 1916. However, after 1916, there was a protracted argument about whether the waves were physical or artefacts of general relativity's coordinate freedom; this debate was not fully addressed until the 1950s.

The LIGO partnership reported on February 11, 2016, that it has directly witnessed gravitational waves for the first time in September 2015. The second gravitational wave observation was made on December 26, 2015, and announced on June 15, 2016.

Gravitational waves convey information that isn't available from other sources. It is possible to acquire a more full knowledge of the source's attributes by integrating observations of a single event recorded using several methods. Multi-messenger astronomy is the term for this. Gravitational waves can also be utilised to observe systems that would otherwise be invisible or nearly difficult to detect. They, for example, offer a one-of-a-kind method of determining the properties of black holes.

Many systems can release gravitational waves, but the source must consist of extremely big particles moving at a considerable fraction of the speed of light to produce detectable signals. A binary of two compact items serves as the primary source.

Some examples of systems are Compact binaries made up of two stellar-mass objects that orbit each other closely, such as white dwarfs, neutron stars, or black holes.

Other potential sources, in addition to binaries, include:Supernovae produce high-frequency bursts of gravitational waves, which LIGO and Virgo could detect.If they have axial asymmetry, rotating neutron stars can produce continuous high-frequency waves.Inflation or a phase transition are examples of early universe activities.If cosmic strings actually exist, they may also release gravitational radiation.The existence of cosmic strings would be confirmed if these gravitational waves were discovered.

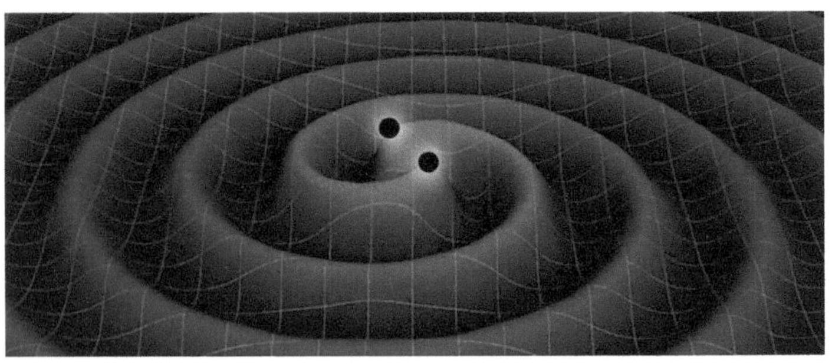

Rotating neutron stars produce continuous high-frequency waves

Gravitational waves only have a minor interaction with matter. This is why they are so tough to spot. It also means that, unlike electromagnetic radiation, they can freely flow across the Universe and are not absorbed or scattered. Because gravitational waves may freely flow through matter, gravitational-wave detectors, unlike telescopes, are aimed to examine the entire sky rather than a single field of view. Some detectors are more sensitive in some directions than others, which is one of the reasons why having a network of detectors is advantageous. Due of the modest number of detectors, directionalization is also weak.

Gravitational-wave observations complement electromagnetic-spectrum observations. These waves also have the potential to provide information in ways that are not possible to obtain through the detection and analysis of electromagnetic waves.

ASTROPHYSICS

CHAPTER TWO

ASTROPHYSICS

Galactic Astronomy

The study of the Milky Way galaxy and all of its contents is known as galactic astronomy. Extragalactic astronomy, on the other hand, is the study of everything outside of our galaxy, including all other galaxies.

Galaxy formation and evolution, which is the overall study of galaxies, their formation, structure, components, dynamics, interactions, and the variety of forms they take, should not be confused with galactic astronomy.

Although key areas of the Milky Way galaxy, to which the Solar System belongs, are blocked from view in visible wavelengths by regions of cosmic dust, it is in many respects the best-studied galaxy. The advent of radio astronomy, infrared astronomy, and sub millimetre astronomy in the twentieth century allowed for the first time the mapping of the Milky Way's gas and dust.

The Milky Way is the galaxy that contains our Solar System, and its name refers to how the galaxy appears in the night sky from Earth: a hazy strip of light generated by stars that cannot be identified individually with the naked eye.

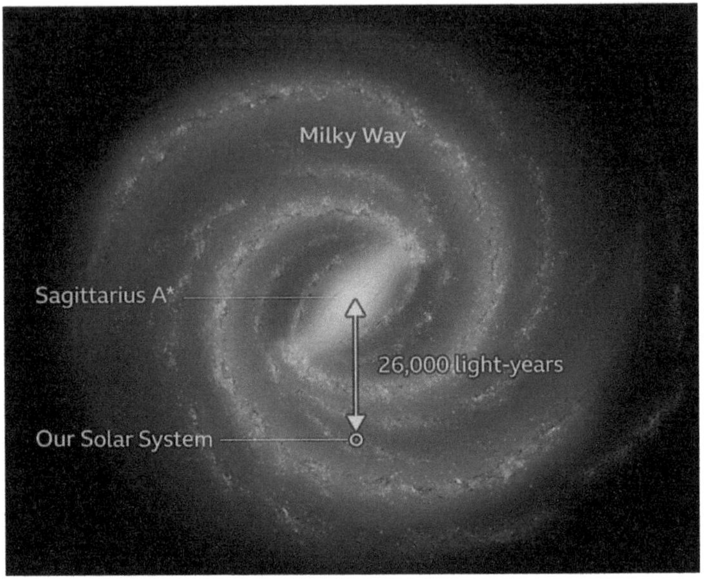

Milky Way galaxy

When Galileo Galilei used a telescope to explore the Milky Way in 1610, he discovered that it is made up of a large number of dim stars. Immanuel Kant suggested (correctly) in a book published in 1755 that the Milky Way might be a spinning body of a massive number of stars kept together by gravitational forces similar to those that hold the Solar System together, but on far bigger scales. From our vantage point inside the disc, the resulting disc of stars would seem as a band on the sky. Some of the nebulae visible in the night sky, according to Wright and Kant, could be independent "galaxies" identical to our own.

The Milky Way and the "extragalactic nebulae" were both referred to as "island universes" by Kant, a concept that was still in use in the 1930s.

William Herschel made the first attempt to define the shape of the Milky Way and the position of the Sun inside it in 1785 by measuring the number of stars in various parts of the visible sky. He drew a diagram depicting the Milky Way's form, including the Solar System at the middle.

Lord Rosse built a new telescope in 1845 and was able to tell the difference between elliptical and spiral-shaped nebulae. He was also able to distinguish specific point sources in some of these nebulae, confirming Kant's prior hypothesis.

In 1904, Jacobus Kapteyn observed that the proper movements of stars were not random, as previously thought; stars could be separated into two streams, travelling in virtually opposing directions. Kapteyn's data was eventually discovered to be the earliest evidence of our galaxy's rotation, which led to Bertil Lindblad and Jan Oort's discovery of galactic rotation.

Most astronomers believed that the Milky Way contained all of the stars in the Universe until the early 1920s. Following the Great Debate of 1920 between astronomers Harlow Shapley and Heber Curtis, Edwin Hubble's investigations revealed that the Milky Way is only one of many galaxies.

The Milky Way is a barred spiral galaxy with a diameter of 100,000–200,000 light-years and an estimated visual diameter of 100,000–200,000 light-years. According to recent calculations, a dark matter region including some visible stars might have a diameter of about 2 million light-years. The Milky Way has multiple satellite galaxies and is a member of the Local Group, which is part of the Virgo Supercluster, which is part of the Laniakea Supercluster.

It is expected that there are 100–400 billion stars and at least that many planets in the galaxy. The Solar System is situated on the inner margin of the Orion Arm, one of the spiral-shaped concentrations of gas and dust, at a distance of roughly 27,000 light-years from the Galactic Center.

The stars in the first 10,000 light-years form a bulge, which is surrounded by one or more bars. Sagittarius A*, a supermassive black hole with a mass of 4.100 (0.034) million solar masses, is at the galactic core. At a distance of around 220 kilometres from the Galactic Center, stars and gases orbit at a rate of approximately 220 kilometres per second.

The steady rotating speed appears to defy Keplerian dynamics, implying that over 90% of the Milky Way's mass remains invisible to observatories because it does neither emit or absorb electromagnetic radiation. "Dark matter" is the name given to this hypothetical mass. At the radius of the Sun, the spinning period is around 240 million years. In extragalactic frames of reference, the Milky Way as a whole moves at a speed of about 600 kilometres per second. The Milky Way's earliest stars are nearly as old as the Universe itself, implying that they formed soon after the Big Bang's Dark Ages.

From Earth, the Milky Way appears as a 30° wide hazy bar of white light arching over the night sky. Although all of the individual naked-eye stars in the entire sky are part of the Milky Way Galaxy, the term "Milky Way" is limited to this strip of light when observing the night sky. The light comes from a buildup of unresolved stars and other debris in the galactic plane's direction.

The visible section of the Milky Way's galactic plane, as seen from Earth, covers an area of the sky that contains 30 constellations. The Galactic Center is located in the constellation Sagittarius, which is the brightest in the Milky Way. The hazy ring of white light appears to pass around the galactic anticenter in Auriga from Sagittarius. The band then circles the sky again, returning to Sagittarius, separating the sky into two roughly equal halves.

After the Andromeda Galaxy, the Milky Way is the second-largest galaxy in the Local Group, with a star disc that is around 170,000–200,000 light-years in diameter and 1,000 light-years thick on average.

Dark matter, an unknown and invisible kind of stuff that interacts gravitationally with conventional matter, appears to make up a large portion of the Milky Way's mass. A dark matter halo is thought to extend beyond one hundred kiloparsecs (kpc) from the Galactic Center, spreading out rather equally.

The Milky Way's disc of stars does not have a distinct edge beyond which no stars exist. Rather, as one moves farther from the Milky Way's centre, the density of stars drops. Beyond a radius of around 40,000 light years from the centre, the number of stars per cubic parsec diminishes substantially faster with radius for unknown reasons.

The interstellar medium and stars in the Milky Way's disc are structured into four spiral arms outside the gravitational effect of the Galactic bar. H II areas and molecular clouds show that spiral arms have a larger density of interstellar gas and dust than the Galactic average, as well as a higher concentration of star formation.The spiral structure of the Milky Way is unknown, and the nature of the Milky Way's arms is also unknown.

The Scutum–Centaurus arm and the Carina–Sagittarius arm both have tangent points inside the Sun's orbit around the Milky Way's core. Counting the stars at the tangent point would reveal if these arms have a higher density of stars than the average density of stars in the Galactic disc.

Two surveys of near-infrared light, which is sensitive to red giants and is unaffected by dust extinction, found the predicted overabundance in the Scutum–Centaurus arm but not in the Carina–Sagittarius arm: the Scutum–Centaurus arm contains approximately 30% more red giants than would be expected in the absence of a spiral arm.

According to this observation, the Milky Way has just two major star arms: the Perseus arm and the Scutum–Centaurus arm. The rest of the arms have a lot of gas but no ancient stars. Astronomers discovered in December 2013 that the distribution of young stars and star-forming areas matched the Milky Way's four-arm spiral description. As a result, old stars appear to trace two spiral arms, while gas and young stars appear to trace four spiral arms. The reason for this apparent disparity is unknown.

The Milky Way's stars and gas move at varying rates around its centre, so the rotation period varies depending on where you look. The orbital speed of most stars in the Milky Way does not rely substantially on their distance from the centre, as is typical in spiral galaxies. The normal star orbital speed is between 210 10 km/s (470,000 22,000 mph) away from the core bulge or outer rim. As a result, the normal star's orbital period is merely proportionate to the length of the journey traversed. This is in contrast to the scenario in the Solar System, where two-body gravitational dynamics rule and different orbits have considerably varied velocities.

The Milky Way and the Andromeda Galaxy are a pair of large spiral galaxies that belong to the Local Group, a cluster of 50 galaxies surrounded by a Local Void, which is part of the Local Sheetand thus the Virgo Supercluster.

Measurements using the Very Long Baseline Array in 2009 found velocities as large as 254 km/s (570,000 mph) for stars at the outer edge of the Milky Way.Because the orbital velocity depends on the total mass inside the orbital radius, this suggests that the Milky Way is more massive, roughly equaling the mass of Andromeda Galaxy.

Both gravitational microlensing and planetary transit studies suggest that there are at least as many planets tied to stars as stars in the Milky Way, and microlensing measurements suggest that there are more rogue planets than stars. According to a January 2013 investigation of the five-planet star system Kepler-32 by the Kepler satellite observatory, the Milky Way has at least one planet per star, resulting in 100–400 billion planets. According to a January 2013 analysis of Kepler data, the Milky Way has at least 17 billion Earth-sized exoplanets.

Based on data from the Kepler satellite mission, astronomers estimated that there could be as many as 40 billion Earth-sized planets orbiting in the habitable zones of Sun-like stars and red dwarfs within the Milky Way on November 4, 2013. It's possible that 11 billion of these planets are orbiting Sun-like stars. According to a 2016 study, the nearest exoplanet may be 4.2 light-years away, circling the red dwarf Proxima Centauri.

The number of such Earth-sized planets may be greater than the number of gas giants. Exocomets, or comets that exist outside of the Solar System, have also been discovered and may be frequent in the Milky Way. More recently, in November 2020, it was projected that the Milky Way Galaxy contains about 300 million livable exoplanets.

According to a simulation published in 2011, the Milky Way's spiral arm structure was formed as a result of numerous collisions with the Sagittarius Dwarf Elliptical

Galaxy.The Milky Way is thought to have two spiral patterns: an inner one, produced by the Sagittarius arm, that rotates quickly, and an outer one, formed by the Carina and Perseus arms, that rotates slowly and has tightly coiled arms. The outer pattern would create an outer pseudoring, and the two patterns would be joined by the Cygnus arm, according to computer simulations of the dynamics of the different spiral arms.

The structure of the Milky Way has been enhanced by discoveries made in the early twenty-first century. With the discovery that the Andromeda Galaxy's (M31) disc extends much farther than previously thought, the possibility of the Milky Way's disc extending further is apparent, as evidenced by the discovery of the Outer Arm extension of the Cygnus Arm and a similar extension of the Scutum–Centaurus Arm. The discovery of the Sagittarius Dwarf Elliptical Galaxy coincided with the discovery of a galactic debris ribbon, as the dwarf's polar orbit and interaction with the Milky Way tear it apart.

The Sloan Digital Sky Survey of the northern sky reveals a massive and diffuse structure within the Milky Way that does not appear to fit current models. The cluster of stars rises almost perpendicular to the plane of the Milky Way's spiral arms. A dwarf galaxy is merging with the Milky Way, according to the most likely explanation. This galaxy, tentatively dubbed the Virgo Stellar Stream, is located around 30,000 light-years away in the direction of Virgo.

A gaseous halo containing a substantial volume of hot gas has been discovered by the Chandra X-ray Observatory, XMM-Newton, and Suzaku, in addition to the stellar halo. The halo is hundreds of thousands of light-years in diameter, significantly larger than the stellar halo and close to the distance between the Large and Small Magellanic

Clouds. This hot halo has a mass that is approximately equal to that of the Milky Way.

Individual stars in the Milky Way can have their ages determined by measuring the amount of long-lived radioactive elements like thorium-232 and uranium-238 and comparing the results to estimates of their original abundance, a technique known as nucleocosmochronology.

Astronomers announced the finding of one of the universe's earliest stars in November 2018. 2MASS J18082002-5104378 B is a tiny ultra metal-poor (UMP) star that is possibly one of the first stars. It is about 13.5 billion years old and is made almost exclusively of components released from the Big Bang. The discovery of the star in our galaxy shows that it is at least 3 billion years older than previously assumed.

Several individual stars in the Milky Way's halo have been discovered with ages that are quite near to the Universe's 13.80-billion-year age. HE 1523-0901, a star in the galactic halo, was estimated to be 13.2 billion years old in 2007.

This measurement set a lower limit on the Milky Way's age because it was the oldest known object in the Milky Way at the time. The relative intensities of spectral lines induced by the presence of thorium and other elements formed by the R-process were measured using the UV-Visual Echelle Spectrograph of the Very Large Telescope. The line strengths produce abundances of various elemental isotopes, which can be used to calculate the star's age using nucleocosmochronology.

The stars in the galaxy's bulge are around 12.8 billion years old, according to measurements using adaptive optics to adjust for Earth's atmospheric distortion.Nucleocosmochronology has also been used to estimate the age of stars in the galactic thin disc.

According to research published in 2014, the Milky Way's satellite galaxies are arranged in a vast disc and orbit in the same direction. The satellite galaxies should develop in dark matter halos, and they should be widely spread and travelling in random directions, according to mainstream cosmology. This disparity has yet to be completely explained.

The previously inexplicable warp in the disc of the Milky Way has now been mapped and discovered to be a ripple or vibration brought up by the Large and Small Magellanic Clouds as they orbit the Milky Way, creating vibrations when they pass across its boundaries, according to researchers in January 2006. These two galaxies, which make up around 2% of the Milky Way's mass, were previously thought to be too small to have an impact on the Milky Way. The velocity of these two galaxies, however, causes a dark matter wake in a computer model, amplifying their influence on the bigger Milky Way.

According to current measurements, the Andromeda Galaxy is approaching us at a speed of 100 to 140 km/s (220,000 to 310,000 mph). Depending on the contribution of unknown lateral components to the galaxies' relative speed, an Andromeda–Milky Way collision could occur in 3 to 4 billion years. Individual stars are unlikely to collide if they collide; instead, the two galaxies will combine to form a single elliptical galaxy or possibly a massive disc galaxy over the course of around a billion years.New photos of the galactic centre were released by NASA in May 2021, based on surveys from the Chandra X-ray Observatory and other telescopes.

Extragalactic astronomy

The discipline of astronomy concerned with objects outside the Milky Way galaxy is known as extragalactic astronomy. The galaxies of the Local Group, which are close enough to allow highly precise examinations of their contents (e.g. supernova remnants, star associations), are among the closest extragalactic objects.

Extragalactic astronomy contains objects at the boundary of the observable cosmos, as instrumentation has developed, distant objects may now be examined in greater detail. Research into faraway galaxies (beyond our local group) is important for understanding features of the cosmos such as galaxy evolution and Active Galactic Nuclei (AGN), which provide insight into physical processes such as supermassive black hole accretion and the presence of dark matter.

Astronomers and physicists can research effects of General Relativity such as gravitational lensing and gravitational waves that are otherwise hard or virtually impossible to examine on a galactic scale,thanks to extragalactic astronomy.

Galaxy cluster

A galaxy cluster, also known as a cluster of galaxies, is a formation made up of hundreds to thousands of galaxies held together by gravity. They are the universe's largest known gravitationally bound formations, and they were thought to be the universe's largest known structures until superclusters were discovered in the 1980s. The intracluster medium is one of the most important characteristics of clusters (ICM). The ICM is made up of hot gas that exists between galaxies.The Virgo Cluster, Fornax Cluster, Hercules Cluster, and Coma Cluster are all notable galaxy clusters in the surrounding Universe. The Great Attractor, which is dominated by the Norma Cluster, is a vast cluster of galaxies large enough to influence the local expansion of the Universe.

Cluster of Galaxies

Gravitational redshift

Radek Wojtak of the Niels Bohr Institute at the University of Copenhagen used galaxy clusters to verify predictions of general relativity, such as energy loss from light fleeing a gravitational field. Because gravity is stronger in the centre of a galaxy cluster, photons emitted from the centre should lose more energy than photons emitted from the periphery. The wavelength of light emitted from the centre of a cluster is longer than that of light emitted from the perimeter. Gravitational redshift is the term for this phenomenon. Wojtak was able to analyse the parameters of gravitational redshift for the distribution of galaxies in clusters using data from 8000 galaxy clusters.He discovered that, as anticipated by general relativity, the light from the clusters was redshifted in proportion to the distance from the cluster's core. The findings also back with the Lambda-Cold Dark Matter model of the Universe, in which the vast majority of the universe is made up of Dark Matter that does not interact with matter.

Gravitational lensing

Galaxy clusters are also employed as gravitational lenses to extend the reach of telescopes due to their strong gravitational potential. Near huge galaxy clusters, gravitational distortion of space-time bends the course of photons, creating a cosmic magnifying glass. This can be done with photons of any wavelength, ranging from optical to X-ray. Because galaxy clusters generate a lot of X-rays, the latter is more challenging. When combining X-ray data with optical data, however, X-ray emition may still be observed. The use of the Phoenix galaxy cluster to view a dwarf galaxy in its early high-energy stages of star formation is one such example.

Supercluster

A supercluster is a massive collection of smaller galaxy clusters or galactic groups that are among the universe's greatest structures. The Milky Way is a member of the Local Group galaxy group, which includes more than 54 galaxies, and is also a member of the Virgo Supercluster, which is a member of the Laniakea Supercluster.

Superclusters, unlike clusters, grow with the Hubble expansion due to their huge size and low density. There are 10 million superclusters in the observable universe, according to estimates.The existence of superclusters implies that galaxies in the Universe are not evenly dispersed; most of them are grouped and clustered, with groups containing dozens of galaxies and clusters holding thousands of galaxies. These groups and clusters, along with additional isolated galaxies, form superclusters, which are much larger formations.

George Abell proposed their existence in his Abell catalogue of galaxy clusters published in 1958. "Second-order clusters," or clusters of clusters, he named them.Superclusters generate huge galaxies known as "filaments," "supercluster complexes," "walls," or "sheets," which can span hundreds of millions to tens of billions of light-years and cover more than 5% of the observable universe.

Supercluster observations can reveal information about the universe's primordial state at the time these superclusters were formed. The directions of galaxies' rotating axes within superclusters may provide insight and knowledge concerning the early formation process of galaxies in the history of the Universe.

Large voids of space, where few galaxies exist, are interspersed throughout superclusters. Superclusters are often separated into galaxy groups and clusters.

Despite the fact that superclusters are considered to be the largest structures in the universe, greater structures have been discovered in surveys, including the Sloan Great Wall.

Intergalactic star

A star that is not gravitationally connected to any galaxy is known as an intergalactic star, sometimes known as an intracluster star or a rogue star. Intergalactic stars, like other stars, are currently assumed to have started in galaxies before being expelled as a result of galaxies merging or a multiple-star system travelling too close to a supermassive black hole, which can be located at the heart of many galaxies.Intergalactic stars are collectively known as the intracluster stellar population, or IC population.

The origin of these stars is still a mystery, but astrophysicists have proposed and published various scientifically viable explanations.The most frequent theory is that when two or more galaxies collide, some stars are thrown out into vast empty intergalactic space.

Although stars are generally found within galaxies, gravitational forces can cause them to be ejected when galaxies collide. Intergalactic stars are thought to have arisen mostly from extremely small galaxies, as it is simpler for stars to escape the gravitational pull of a smaller galaxy than it is for a massive galaxy.

When big galaxies collide, however, some of the gravitational disturbances may cause stars to be expelled. In 2015, a study of supernovae in intergalactic space suggested that the progenitor stars were ejected from their host galaxies during a galactic collision between two giant ellipticals as their supermassive black hole centres merged, implying that the progenitor stars were ejected from their host galaxies during a galactic collision between two giant ellipticals.

Another possibility, which isn't mutually incompatible with the galactic collisions hypothesis, is that intergalactic stars were ejected from their home galaxy by a near encounter with the galaxy's supermassive black hole, if one exists. It's conceivable that the intergalactic star(s) were once part of a multi-star system, with the other stars being sucked into the supermassive black hole and the soon-to-be intergalactic star being accelerated and ejected away at extremely high speeds.

Such an occurrence might conceivably accelerate a star to such high speeds that it becomes a hypervelocity star, allowing it to escape the galaxy's gravitational well. In this regard, model projections from 1988 predict that our Milky Way galaxy's supermassive black hole will expel one star every 100,000 years on average.

In the Virgo cluster of galaxies, the first intergalactic stars were identified. The distance between them and the nearest galaxy is roughly 300,000 light years. Although the actual amount of the intergalactic star population is unknown, it is estimated that they make about 10% of the mass of the Virgo cluster of galaxies on a local scale and most likely, this total outweighs any of its 2500 galaxies.

In the Virgo cluster of galaxies, the Hubble Space Telescope spotted a huge number of intergalactic stars in 1997. In the Fornax cluster of galaxies, scientists discovered another clump of intergalactic stars later in the 1990s.

A diffuse glow from the intergalactic medium, although of unknown origin, was observed in the late 2000s. It was claimed and demonstrated in 2012 that it could have come from intergalactic stars. Following observations and research, the subject was expanded upon, and the diffuse extragalactic background radiation was described in greater detail.

More than 675 stars have been discovered at the Milky Way's edge, between the Andromeda Galaxy and the Milky Way, according to Vanderbilt astronomers. They claim that these stars are hypervelocity intergalactic stars ejected from the galactic centre of the Milky Way.

These stars are red giants with a high metallicity, a measure of the proportion of chemical elements other than hydrogen and helium within a star that indicates an inner galactic origin, because stars outside galaxies' discs tend to have low metallicity and are older.Hundreds of thousands of light-years from the nearest star or galaxy, some recently discovered supernovae have been proven to have erupted.

The majority of intergalactic star candidates discovered in the Milky Way's vicinity appear to have originated in the Milky Way disc or elsewhere, rather than in the Galactic Center.

Intergalactic dust

Cosmic dust found between galaxies in intergalactic space is known as intergalactic dust. Evidence for intergalactic dust was first proposed in 1949, and research into it developed during the late twentieth century. The spread of interplanetary dust varies dramatically. Intergalactic distance measurements, such as those to supernovae and quasars in other galaxies, may be affected by the dust.

Intergalactic dust can generate intergalactic dust clouds, which have been observed surrounding several galaxies since the 1960s. The Okroy cloud was one of at least four intergalactic dust clouds identified within several megaparsecs of the Milky Way galaxy during the 1980s.

NASA reported in February 2014 that their database for tracking polycyclic aromatic hydrocarbons (PAHs) in the universe has been considerably enhanced. According to scientists, PAHs may account for more than 20% of the carbon in the cosmos, making them potential starting ingredients for the genesis of life. PAHs appear to have developed as early as two billion years after the Big Bang, are found everywhere over the universe, and are linked to the formation of new stars and exoplanets.

Extragalactic planet

A star-bound planet or rogue planet located outside of the Milky Way Galaxy is known as an extragalactic planet, sometimes known as an extragalactic exoplanet or an extroplanet. Due to the vast distances between such worlds, immediate detection would be extremely difficult.

Indirect evidence, on the other hand, suggests that such planets exist. Despite this, the most distant known planets are SWEEPS-11 and SWEEPS-04, which are located in the constellation Sagittarius and are around 27,710 light-years from the Sun, whereas the Milky Way is between 100,000 and 180,000 light-years in diameter. This suggests that even galaxy planets beyond that distance have yet to be discovered.

R. E. Schild discovered a microlensing event in the Twin Quasar gravitational lensing system in the "A" lobe of the lensed quasar in 1996. The event is thought to have been triggered by a 3-Earth-mass planet in the lensing galaxy YGKOW G1. This was the first candidate for an extragalactic planet to be announced. However, because this was a one-time chance alignment, it is not a reproducible finding. This planet is estimated to be 4 billion light years away.

A team of scientists has discovered a possible extragalactic exoplanet in Andromeda, the Milky Way's nearest major galactic neighbour, using gravitational microlensing. The lensing pattern is consistent with a star having a smaller companion, PA-99-N2, weighing around 6.34 times Jupiter's mass. This is the first confirmed planet in the Andromeda Galaxy.

In 2018, astrophysicists from the University of Oklahoma discovered, for the first time, a population of unbound planets between stars with masses ranging from Lunar to Jovian masses in the lensing galaxy that microlenses quasar RX J1131-1231.

The discovery of a candidate planet circling the high-mass X-ray binary M51-ULS-1 in the Whirlpool Galaxy was announced in September 2020. Eclipses of the X-ray source, which consists of a stellar remnant, possibly a neutron star or a black hole, and a big star, most likely a B-type supergiant, detected the planet. The planet would be slightly smaller than Saturn and orbit at a distance of tens of astronomical units (AU). In October 2021, M51-ULS-1b was announced in Nature as the first known extragalactic planet candidate.

Even though the star has been absorbed by our own galaxy, the European Southern Observatory (ESO) may have detected a planet with a mass of at least 1.25 times that of Jupiter orbiting a star of extragalactic origin. HIP 13044 is a star in the southern constellation Fornax that is about 2,000 light years away. It is part of the Helmi stream of stars, which is a remnant of a tiny galaxy that collided with and was swallowed by the Milky Way around 6 billion years ago.

Stellar Astronomy

Our comprehension of the Universe depends on the study of stars and stellar evolution. The internal astrophysics of stars has been determined through observation and theoretical understanding, as well as computer simulations.Giant molecular clouds, which are dense areas of dust and gas, are where stars form. Cloud pieces can collapse under the pull of gravity to produce a protostar when they are destabilised. Nuclear fusion will be triggered by a sufficiently dense and hot core area, resulting in the formation of a main-sequence star.

In the centres of stars, almost all elements heavier than hydrogen and helium were formed. The characteristics of the resulting star are largely determined by its initial mass. The more massive a star is, the brighter it is and the faster its hydrogen fuel is converted to helium in its core. The hydrogen fuel is totally transformed to helium over time, and the star starts to evolve. Helium fusion necessitates a greater core temperature. A star with a high core temperature will expand its core density while pushing its outer layers outward.

The ensuing red giant, generated by the growing outer layers, lives only a short time before the helium fuel in the core is depleted. As they fuse ever heavier elements, very massive stars can go through a succession of evolutionary phases.Stars with masses higher than eight times that of the Sun explode as core collapse supernovae, whereas smaller stars blow off their outer layers and leave behind an inert core in the form of a white dwarf. A planetary nebula is formed by the ejection of the outer layers.A dense neutron star or, if the stellar mass was at least three times that of the Sun, a black hole is the remnant of a supernova.

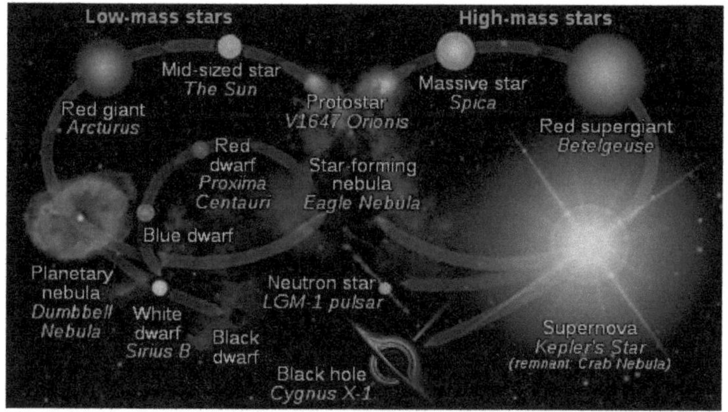

Stellar evolution of low-mass and high-mass stars

Closely circling binary stars can take more complicated evolutionary pathways, such as mass transfer to a white dwarf companion, which could result in a supernova explosion. All new stars (and their planetary systems) would be born from hydrogen and helium alone if planetary nebulae and supernovae did not transfer the "metals" produced in the star by fusion to the interstellar medium.

Stellar evolution

The process through which a star evolves over time is known as stellar evolution. The lifespan of a star varies greatly depending on its mass, ranging from a few million years for the most massive to trillions of years for the least massive, which is much longer than the universe's history.

All stars are born from the collapse of gas and dust clouds known as nebulae or molecular clouds. These proto stars settle into a state of equilibrium over millions of years, creating what is known as a main-sequence star.

For the most part, a star is powered by nuclear fusion. The energy is initially created by hydrogen atom fusion at the core of a main-sequence star. Stars like the Sun begin to fuse hydrogen along a spherical shell surrounding the core as the abundance of atoms at the core changes to helium. The star grows in size as a result of this process, passing through the sub giant stage before reaching the red-giant stage.

Stars with a mass of at least half that of the Sun can start to create energy by fusing helium at their core, whereas larger stars can fuse heavier elements in a series of concentric shells. When a star like the Sun runs out of nuclear fuel, its core collapses into a compact white dwarf, while the outer layers are ejected as planetary nebulae. As their inert iron cores collapse into an extraordinarily dense neutron star or black hole, stars with ten or more times the mass of the Sun can explode in a supernova.

The life of a single star is not used to study stellar evolution since most stellar changes are too slow to be seen, even over millennia. Instead, astrophysicists learn about star evolution by monitoring a large number of stars at different stages of their lives and simulating stellar structure with computer models.

Star Formation

The gravitational collapse of a massive molecular cloud is the beginning of stellar evolution. Giant molecular clouds are 100 light-years broad (9.51014 km) and may hold up to 6,000,000 solar masses (1.21037 kg). A massive molecular cloud breaks up into smaller and smaller fragments as it crashes. The compressing gas releases gravitational potential energy as heat in each of these shards. A fragment condenses into a revolving ball of superhot gas known as a protostar as its temperature and pressure rise.

As it reaches its full mass, a protostar continues to grow by accreting gas and dust from the molecular cloud, eventually becoming a pre-main-sequence star.Its mass determines its future evolution. The mass of the Sun is sometimes used as a comparison: 1.0 M (2.01030 kg) equals 1 solar mass.

Orion A molecular cloud

Because protostars are engulfed in dust, they are more visible at infrared wavelengths. The Wide-field Infrared Survey Explorer (WISE) observations have been particularly useful in revealing a number of galactic protostars and their parent star clusters.

Protostars with masses of less than 0.08 M (1.61029 kg) never achieve temperatures high enough to initiate hydrogen nuclear fusion. The core temperature of a more massive protostar will eventually approach 10 million kelvin, triggering the proton–proton chain reaction and allowing hydrogen to fuse into deuterium and then helium.

The carbon–nitrogen–oxygen fusion reaction (CNO cycle) generates a major share of the energy generation in stars with a mass of slightly more than 1 M (2.01030 kg). When nuclear fusion begins, the star quickly enters a hydrostatic equilibrium, in which the energy supplied by the core maintains a high gas pressure, balancing the star's mass and preventing further gravitational collapse. As a result, the star swiftly evolves to a stable condition, kicking off the main-sequence phase of its existence.

Small, cold, low-mass red dwarfs fuse hydrogen slowly and can last hundreds of billions of years or more on the main sequence, whereas big, hot O-type stars can only last a few million years. A mid-sized yellow dwarf star, like the Sun, will last roughly 10 billion years on the main sequence. The Sun's main sequence lifespan is considered to be near the middle.

When the star's core runs out of hydrogen, the star begins to develop away from the main sequence. The core contracts until either the electron degeneracy pressure becomes sufficient to fight gravity or the core becomes hot enough (about 100 MK) for helium fusion to commence without the outward radiation pressure generated by hydrogen fusion to counteract the force of gravity. The mass of the star determines which of these events occurs first.

What happens after a low-mass star stops producing energy through fusion has not been directly observed; the universe is roughly 13.8 billion years old, which is significantly shorter time (by many orders of magnitude) than it takes for fusion to stop in such stars. Recent astrophysical simulations imply that red dwarfs with a mass of 0.1 M might survive on the main sequence for six to twelve trillion years, steadily growing in warmth and luminosity, before slowly collapsing into a white dwarf.

Because the entire star is a convection zone, such stars will not become red giants and will not create a degenerate helium core with a shell burning hydrogen. Instead, hydrogen fusion will continue until nearly the entire star is made of helium. Stars that are slightly more massive expand into red giants, but their helium cores aren't huge enough to achieve the temperatures required for helium fusion, so they never reach the red-giant branch's tip. When the hydrogen shell burns up, these stars, like post-asymptotic-giant-branch (AGB) stars, travel directly off the red-giant branch to become white dwarfs, albeit at a lower brightness.

A star with an initial mass of roughly 0.6 M can achieve temperatures high enough to fuse helium, and these "mid-sized" stars progress beyond the red-giant stage of evolution.

During two phases of their post-main-sequence evolution, mid-sized stars become red giants: red-giant-branch stars with inert cores made of helium and hydrogen-burning shells, and asymptotic-giant-branch stars with inert cores made of carbon and helium-burning shells inside the hydrogen-burning shells. Stars spend a period on the horizontal branch with a helium-fusing core between these two stages. Many of these helium-fusing stars cluster as K-type giants near the cold end of the horizontal branch, and are known as red clump giants.

When a star's hydrogen supply in its core runs out, it exits the main sequence and starts fusing hydrogen in a shell outside the core. As the shell produces more helium, the core grows in mass. This can last for few million to one or two billion years, depending on the mass of the helium core, with the star expanding and cooling at a similar or slightly lower brightness than its main sequence state. In stars around the mass of the sun, the core eventually degenerates, whereas in more massive stars, the outer layers cool enough to become opaque.Either of these changes raises the temperature of the hydrogen shell and increases the star's brightness, causing the star to expand onto the red-giant branch.

In huge stars, the core is already large enough at the start of the hydrogen burning shell for helium to ignite before electron degeneracy pressure becomes a problem. As a result, these stars do not brighten as drastically as lower-mass stars when they expand and cool; yet, they were more luminous on the main sequence and evolve to extraordinarily luminous supergiants. Their cores become so massive that electron degeneracy can no longer support them, and they finally collapse to form a neutron star or black hole.

Extremely massive stars with masses greater than 40 M, which are very luminous and thus have very fast stellar winds, lose mass so quickly due to radiation pressure that they tend to strip off their own envelopes before expanding to become red supergiants, and thus retain extremely high surface temperatures and a blue-white colour from main-sequence time onwards. Because the outer layers would be expelled by the strong radiation, the present generation's largest stars are around 100-150 M.As material from hydrogen fusion outside the core accretes, the core of a massive star, defined as the region depleted of hydrogen, grows hotter and denser. The core of sufficiently large stars reaches temperatures and densities high enough for the alpha process to fuse carbon and heavier elements.

A star's core is mostly made up of carbon and oxygen at the end of helium fusion. Carbon ignites and fuses to generate neon, sodium, and magnesium in stars heavier than around 8 M. Smaller stars may partially ignite carbon, but they are unable to fully fuse the carbon before electron degeneracy occurs, and these stars will eventually leave an oxygen-rich remnant. White dwarf -neon-magnesium.

The actual mass limit for full carbon burning is 8-9 M, depending on numerous factors such as metallicity and the detailed mass lost on the asymptotic giant branch. The core of these stars reaches roughly 2.5 M when carbon burning is complete, which is hot enough for heavier elements to combine. Neon begins to collect electrons before oxygen begins to fuse, causing neon to burn. This mechanism is unstable for stars with masses of 8-12 M, resulting in uncontrolled fusion and an electron capture explosion.

The fusing of neon occurs without a runaway deflagration in more massive stars. This is followed by full oxygen and silicon burning, resulting in a core primarily made up of iron-peak components. Shells of lighter elements surround the core, which are still undergoing fusion. Because complete fusion of a carbon core to an iron core takes only a few hundred years, the outer layers of the star are unable to respond, and the star's appearance remains mostly unchanged.

Due to multiple corrections for relativistic effects, entropy, charge, and the surrounding envelope, the iron core increases until it reaches an effective Chandrasekhar mass, which is higher than the formal Chandrasekhar mass. In the most massive red supergiants, the effective Chandrasekhar mass for an iron core ranges from roughly

1.34 M to more than 1.8 M. When this mass is attained, electrons are trapped in the iron-peak nuclei, and the core can no longer support itself. The star is killed when the core collapses, either as a supernova or as a direct collapse to a black hole.

Supernova

When the core of a big star collapses, it forms a neutron star or, if the Tolman–Oppenheimer–Volkoff limit is exceeded, a black hole. Some of the gravitational potential energy released by this core collapse is converted into a Type Ib, Type Ic, or Type II supernova through an unknown method. The core collapse is known to cause a tremendous influx of neutrinos, as seen in supernova SN 1987A. The extremely energetic neutrinos fragment some nuclei; some of their energy is consumed in the release of nucleons, including neutrons, and some of their energy is converted into heat and kinetic energy, amplifying the shock wave caused by the rebound of some of the infalling material from the collapse of the core .

Additional neutrons may be produced via electron capture in highly dense regions of the infalling materials. Because part of the rebounding matter gets hit by neutrons, some of its nuclei are captured, resulting in a spectrum of heavier-than-iron material that includes radioactive elements up to uranium. Although non-exploding red giants can produce significant amounts of heavier elements than iron using neutrons released in side reactions of earlier nuclear reactions, the abundance of heavier elements produced in such reactions differs significantly from that produced in a supernova.

Both supernovae and ejection of elements from red giants are necessary to explain the observed abundance of heavy elements and isotopes, as neither abundance matches that found in the Solar System.

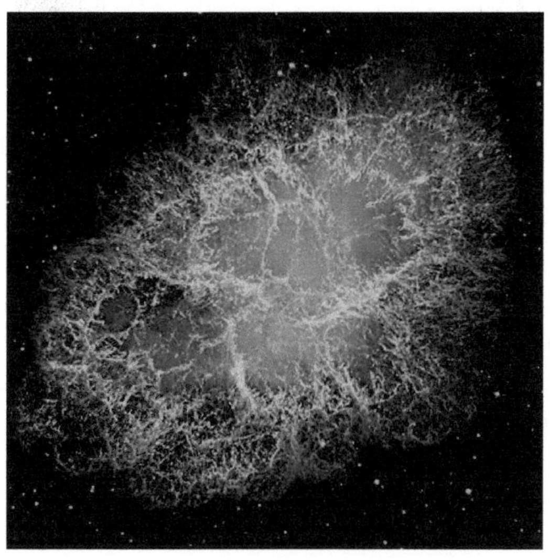

The Crab Nebula, remnants of a supernova that was first observed around 1050 AD

The energy transferred from the core's collapse to rebounding material not only creates heavy elements, but also accelerates them well beyond their escape velocity, resulting in a Type Ib, Type Ic, or Type II supernova. Although current computer models of Type Ib, Type Ic, and Type II supernovae account for some of the energy transfer, they are not able to account for enough energy transfer to produce the observed material ejection.

Neutrino oscillations, on the other hand, may play a significant role in the energy transfer problem because they alter the energy available in a specific flavour of neutrinos as well as other general-relativistic effects on neutrinos.The collapse of an oxygen-neon-magnesium core may produce a supernova that differs observably in ways other than size from a supernova produced by the collapse of an iron core, according to evidence obtained from analysis of the mass and orbital parameters of binary neutron stars which require two such supernovae.

A supernova with an energy far greater than its gravitational binding energy might entirely destroy today's most massive stars. This unusual phenomenon, which is triggered by pair-instability, leaves no traces of a black hole. Some stars in the past of the universe were much larger than the largest that exist today, and at the conclusion of their existence, they would collapse into a black hole owing to photodisintegration.

Stellar Remnants

Depending on the mass of a star throughout its lifespan, its remnants can adopt one of three forms after it has burned all its fuel supply.

- White dwarf , black dwarfs
- Neutron stars
- Black holes

For a star with a mass of 1 M, the resulting white dwarf has a mass of roughly 0.6 M and is squeezed to about the same volume as the Earth. Because of the Pauli exclusion principle, the inward force of gravity is balanced by the degeneracy pressure of the star's electrons, making white dwarfs stable. Because the electron degeneracy pressure acts as a soft limit to additional compression, white dwarfs with a larger mass have a lower volume for a given chemical composition. The star releases its leftover heat into space for billions of years since it has run out of fuel to burn.

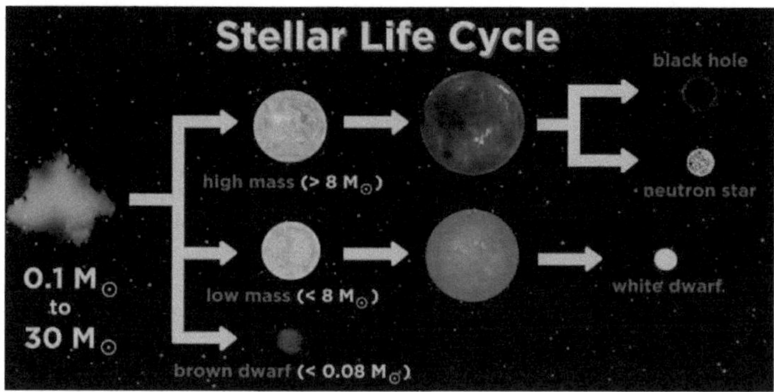

Stellar Life Cycle

When a white dwarf first forms, it is extremely hot, with a surface temperature of more than 100,000 K and an inner temperature substantially higher. It is so hot that for the first 10 million years of its existence, a lot of its energy is lost as neutrinos, but after a billion years, it will have lost most of its energy.

The mass of the white dwarf determines its chemical composition. A star of a few solar masses will ignite carbon fusion to form magnesium, neon, and smaller amounts of other elements, resulting in a white dwarf composed primarily of oxygen, neon, and magnesium, assuming it can lose enough mass to fall below the Chandrasekhar limit and the carbon ignition is not violent enough to blow the star apart in a supernova. A star of the Sun's mass will be unable to spark carbon fusion, resulting in the formation of a white dwarf consisting primarily of carbon and oxygen, with a mass too low to collapse unless matter is supplied later.

A star with a mass less than half that of the Sun will be unable to initiate helium fusion, resulting in a helium-dominated white dwarf. All that remains in the end is a frigid, dark mass known as a black dwarf. However, the cosmos isn't old enough to have any black dwarfs. When the white dwarf's mass exceeds the Chandrasekhar limit, which is 1.4 M for a white dwarf consisting primarily of carbon, oxygen, neon, and/or magnesium, electron degeneracy pressure fails and the star falls owing to electron capture. Depending on the chemical composition and pre-collapse temperature at the centre, this will result in either neutron star collapse or runaway carbon and oxygen ignition.

Higher core temperatures encourage runaway nuclear reactions, which halt core collapse and lead to a Type Ia supernova. Heavier elements favour ongoing core collapse since they require a higher temperature to ignite, because electron capture onto these elements and their fusion products is easier.

Even though the Type II supernova, which marks the death of a big star, has a greater overall energy release, these supernovae may be several times brighter. Because of its instability, no white dwarf with a mass greater than 1.4 M can exist. An initially stable white dwarf may exceed the Chandrasekhar limit due to mass transfer in a binary system.

If a white dwarf forms a tight binary system with another star, hydrogen from the larger partner may accrete around and onto the white dwarf until it becomes hot enough to fuse in a runaway reaction at its surface, although remaining below the Chandrasekhar limit. A nova is the name given to such an explosion.

By volume, atoms are largely electron clouds with very compact nuclei at the centre; if atoms were the size of a football stadium, their nuclei would be dust mites. The pressure of a star core collapsing leads electrons and protons to fuse through electron capture.

Without electrons to keep nuclei apart, neutrons collapse into a dense ball that resembles a huge atomic nucleus, with a thin layer of degenerate matter, primarily iron, atop it unless other matter of differing composition is introduced later. The Pauli exclusion principle, which is similar to electron degeneracy pressure but stronger, prevents the neutrons from being compressed any further.

These stars, also known as neutron stars, are exceedingly tiny (on the order of 10 km in diameter, around the size of a major city) and highly dense. Due to conservation of angular momentum, the period of rotation of neutron stars shortens substantially as they shrink; measured rotational periods of neutron stars range from roughly 1.5 milliseconds (about 600 revolutions per second) to several seconds. We detect a pulse of radiation each revolution when the magnetic poles of these rapidly spinning stars align with the Earth.

Pulsars are the first neutron stars to be discovered, and they were the first neutron stars to be discovered. Though pulsars emit electromagnetic radiation in the form of radio waves, they have also been identified at visible, X-ray, and gamma ray wavelengths.

The neutron degeneracy pressure will be inadequate to prevent collapse below the Schwarzschild radius if the star remnant's mass is high enough. As a result, the star remnant becomes a black hole. The exact mass at which this happens is unknown, however it is currently considered to be between 2 and 3 M.

The theory of general relativity predicts black holes. According to classical general relativity, no matter or information can flow from a black hole's interior to an observer on the outside, while quantum phenomena may allow for exceptions. Both theoretically and via astronomical observation, the existence of black holes in the cosmos is firmly supported.

Because the core-collapse mechanism of a supernova is only partially understood at the moment, it's unclear whether a star can collapse directly to a black hole without producing a visible supernova, or whether some supernovae first form unstable neutron stars before collapsing into black holes; the exact relationship between the initial mass of the star and the final remnant is also unknown. More supernovae and supernova remnants must be studied to resolve these ambiguities.

A stellar evolutionary model is a mathematical model that may be used to calculate the stages of a star's evolution from formation to remnant. The star's mass and chemical composition are used as inputs, with the only limits being its luminosity and surface temperature. The model formulae are based on the star's physical properties, which are commonly assumed to be in hydrostatic equilibrium.

The star's changing condition over time is then determined using extensive computer calculations, providing a table of data that can be used to calculate the star's evolutionary track through the Hertzsprung–Russell diagram.By comparing a star's physical parameters to those of stars on a similar evolutionary track, accurate models may be used to determine a star's current age.

Solar Astronomy

The Sun astronomy, or solar astronomy, is the astronomy of the "star at the core of the Solar System," as portrayed in astronomy.

The Sun is the central star of our Solar System. It's a nearly perfect ball of hot plasma, heated to incandescence at its centre by nuclear fusion reactions and emitting energy mostly as visible light, ultraviolet, and infrared radiation. It is the primary source of energy for life on the planet.

The diameter of the Sun is approximately 1.39 million kilometres (864,000 miles), or 109 times that of the Earth. Its mass is approximately 330,000 times that of Earth, accounting for 99.86 percent of the Solar System's total mass. Hydrogen makes up almost three-quarters of the Sun's mass (73%) and helium (25%) of the rest, with much lesser amounts of heavier elements such as oxygen, carbon, neon, and iron.

The Sun's core fuses around 600 million tonnes of hydrogen into helium every second, converting 4 million tonnes of mass into energy in the process. The Sun's light and heat come from this energy, which takes between 10,000 and 170,000 years to escape the core. When hydrogen fusion in the Sun's core reaches a point where it is no longer in hydrostatic equilibrium, the Sun's core will experience a significant rise in density and temperature, while its outer layers expand, converting the Sun into a red giant. The Sun will eventually grow huge enough to encompass the current orbits of Mercury and Venus, rendering Earth uninhabitable — but not for another five billion years.The Sun is a main-sequence G-type star (G2V). As a result, it is referred regarded as a yellow dwarf.

It arose from the gravitational collapse of matter within an area of a massive molecular cloud about 4.6 billion years ago. The majority of this matter accumulated in the centre, while the rest flattened out into the Solar System's orbiting disc. The central mass became so hot and dense that nuclear fusion began to occur in its core. This process is assumed to be responsible for the formation of practically all stars.

The chemical components hydrogen and helium make up the majority of the Sun. They make up 74.9 percent and 23.8 percent of the Sun's mass in the photosphere, respectively, at this point in its life. All heavier elements, known as metals in astronomy, make up less than 2% of the total mass, with oxygen (approximately 1% of the Sun's mass), carbon (0.3%), neon (0.2%), and iron (0.2%) being the most plentiful.

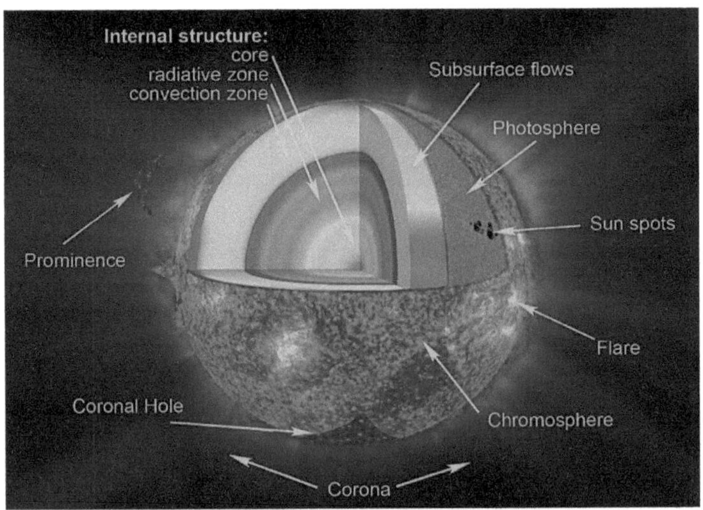

Structure of the Sun

Spectroscopic studies of the Sun advanced in the 19th century, with Joseph von Fraunhofer recording over 600 absorption lines in the spectrum, the strongest of which are now referred to as Fraunhofer lines. The source of the Sun's energy was a key puzzle in the early years of the modern scientific age. Lord Kelvin proposed that the Sun is a slowly cooling liquid entity that radiates heat from within.

Kelvin and Hermann von Helmholtz next proposed a gravitational contraction mechanism to explain the energy output, but the resulting age estimate was just 20 million years, well short of the time span suggested by some geological discoveries at the time, which was at least 300 million years. Joseph Lockyer, the first person to find helium in the solar spectrum, suggested a meteoritic theory for the Sun's creation and evolution in 1890.

NASA's Pioneers 6, 7, 8, and 9, launched between 1959 and 1968, were the first spacecraft designed for long-term observations of the Sun from interplanetary space. These probes orbited the Sun at a similar distance to Earth, taking the first detailed measurements of the solar wind and magnetic field. Pioneer 9 was especially long-lived, delivering data until May 1983.

Two Helios spacecraft and the Skylab Apollo Telescope Mount supplied substantial new data on solar wind and the solar corona to scientists in the 1970s. The Helios 1 and 2 missions were joint projects between the United States and Germany that researched the solar wind from an orbit that took them within Mercury's orbit at perihelion. The Apollo Telescope Mount was a solar observatory module that was operated by astronauts on the Skylab space station, which was launched by NASA in 1973. The solar transition area and ultraviolet radiation from the solar corona were observed for the first time by Skylab. The first observations of coronal mass ejections, then known as "coronal transients," and coronal holes, now known to be intimately related with the solar wind, were among the discoveries.

NASA launched the Solar Maximum Mission in 1980. During a period of high solar activity and solar luminosity, this spacecraft was meant to study gamma rays, X-rays, and UV radiation from solar flares. However, just a few months after launch, an electrical malfunction forced the probe into hibernation mode, where it remained for the next three years. The satellite was collected and repaired by the Space Shuttle Challenger mission STS-41C in 1984 before being re-released into orbit. Before re-entering Earth's atmosphere in June 1989, the Solar Maximum Mission took thousands of photos of the solar corona.

The Yohkoh (Sunbeam) satellite, launched in 1991, detected solar flares at X-ray wavelengths. Scientists were able to identify numerous different types of flares using data from the mission, demonstrating that the corona outside of regions of peak activity was far more dynamic and energetic than previously thought. Yohkoh tracked the Sun through a whole solar cycle until going into standby mode in 2001 after losing its lock on the Sun due to an annular eclipse. In 2005, it was destroyed by atmospheric re-entry.

The Solar and Heliospheric Observatory, designed jointly by the European Space Agency and NASA and launched on December 2, 1995, is one of the most important solar missions to date. In October 2009, a mission extension through 2012 was accepted, which was originally supposed to be a two-year mission. The Solar Dynamics Observatory (SDO), a follow-up mission, was launched in February 2010 as a result of its success. Since its debut, SOHO has provided a steady picture of the Sun at various wavelengths since it is located at the Lagrangian point between Earth and the Sun when the gravitational pull from each is equal.

All of these satellites saw the Sun from the plane of the ecliptic, allowing them to focus on its equatorial regions. In 1990, NASA launched the Ulysses mission to examine the Sun's polar regions. It first went to Jupiter in order to "slingshot" into an orbit well above the plane of the ecliptic. Once in its planned orbit, Ulysses began observing the solar wind and magnetic field strength at high solar latitudes, discovering that the solar wind from high latitudes was moving at about 750 km/s, which was slower than expected, and that large magnetic waves were emerging from high latitudes, scattering galactic cosmic rays.

Spectroscopic research have revealed the abundances of elements in the photosphere, but the composition of the Sun's interior is less well understood. Genesis, a solar wind sample return mission, was created to allow scientists to measure the composition of solar material directly.

In October 2006, the Solar Terrestrial Relations Observatory (STEREO) mission was launched. Two identical spacecraft were launched into orbits that caused them to gradually pull ahead of and fall behind Earth, respectively. The Sun and solar events such as coronal mass ejections can now be viewed in stereoscopic mode.

The Parker Solar Probe was launched in 2018 atop a Delta IV Heavy rocket and will reach a perigee of 0.046 AU in 2025, making it the first spacecraft to fly down into the solar corona and the closest-orbiting manmade satellite.

The Indian Space Research Organisation has launched Aditya, a 100-kilogram satellite. A coronagraph will be its primary instrument for researching the dynamics of the solar corona.Solar Astronomy intersect with many fields like magnetohydrodynamics, seismology, Plasma Physics, space weather.

Magnetohydrodynamics

The study of the magnetic characteristics and behaviour of electrically conducting fluids is known as magnetohydrodynamics -MHD; alternatively magneto-fluid dynamics or hydromagnetics.

MHD is also in charge of the solar wind. The solar wind is a stream of charged particles discharged from the Sun's corona, or upper atmosphere. Electrons, protons, and alpha particles with kinetic energies between 0.5 and 10 keV make up the majority of this plasma.

The solar wind plasma also contains a mixture of materials found in the solar plasma, including trace amounts of heavy ions and atomic nuclei such as C, N, O, Ne, Mg, Si, S, and Fe, as well as trace amounts of heavy ions and atomic nuclei such as C, N, O, Ne, Mg, Si, S, and Fe.

Large, fast-moving blasts of plasma known as coronal mass ejections, or CMEs, can disrupt both the fast and slow solar wind. A discharge of magnetic energy at the Sun causes CMEs. CMEs are referred to as "solar storms" or "space storms."

Coronal Mass Ejections

Solar flares, which are another manifestation of magnetic energy release at the Sun, are sometimes, but not always, related with them. CMEs create shock waves in the heliosphere's thin plasma, which launch electromagnetic waves and accelerate particles mainly protons and electrons to form ionising radiation showers that precede the CME.On October 25, 2006, NASA launched STEREO, a pair of nearly-identical spacecraft capable of producing the first stereoscopic photos of CMEs and other solar activity data from far distant places in their orbits.The Parker Solar Probe was launched on August 12, 2018, with the goal of determining the mechanisms that accelerate and transport energetic particles, i.e. the solar wind's origins.

CMEs occasionally reach Earth and cause a variety of problems in the space environment, where a large amount of societal infrastructure is in use. As a result, estimating the time of arrival of CMEs is an important topic in space weather research.

Many research have used empirical models and global magnetohydrodynamic (MHD) simulations of the heliosphere to predict CME arrival. The background solar wind is calculated using magnetic field measurements from the solar surface and empirical models of solar wind speed are used in these simulations. The CMEs are then approximated as simple structures such as cones in the simulations.

Helioseismology

Douglas Gough developed the term helioseismology to describe the study of the Sun's structure and motion through its oscillations. Global helioseismology, which investigates the Sun's resonant modes directly, and local helioseismology, which studies the propagation of the component waves near the Sun's surface, are the two branches of the current field.

A lot of scientific advances have been attributed to helioseismology. The most notable was demonstrating that the Sun's anticipated neutrino flow could not be explained by faults in stellar models and must instead be a particle physics problem.Helioseismology also enabled for precise measurements of the Sun's gravitational potential's quadrupole (and higher-order) moments, which are consistent with General Relativity.

Continuous monitoring of the Sun benefits helioseismology the most, which began with unbroken observations at the South Pole throughout the austral summer. Furthermore, helioseismologists have been able to analyse changes in the Sun's structure over decades thanks to observations spanning numerous solar cycles. Global telescope networks like as the Global Oscillations Network Group (GONG) and the Birmingham Solar Oscillations Network (BiSON), which have been in operation for decades, have enabled these research.

Plasma Physics

There is very little hydrogen and helium gas in the Sun and stars. The atoms are virtually entirely ionised into hydrogen ions and helium ions due to the high temperatures, resulting in a plasma. These ions are not the same as gaseous atoms, and they behave differently.

The Sun's atoms are mostly ionised. This is especially true in the hot, dense interior, where almost all hydrogen and helium atoms have been ionised. Plasma is the name for a highly ionised gas like this. Although the Sun is sometimes described as a gaseous body, a more accurate definition is that it is formed of plasma. The plasma in this scenario is made up of hydrogen and helium ions, as well as the electrons released when those ions were created.The heliospheric current sheet is formed by the action of the Sun's spinning magnetic field on plasma in the interplanetary medium, which separates regions with magnetic fields pointing in various directions. The strength of the Sun's magnetic field near the Earth's orbit is also due to plasma in the interplanetary medium.Current loops in solar flares, current sheets in the Solar Corona, and general twisting electric current helicity in the solar atmosphere are all known to be caused by the Sun's and stars' high density plasma.

By simulating several of the sun's features in tests on Earth, Kristian Birkeland's Terella experiments provided more evidence for electrical activity on the sun. In a big vacuum-box, a magnetic globe served as an electrically charged cathode. Many characteristics of the sun, including the corona, plasma torus, sunspots, and the so-called magnetic reconnection, which is more accurately defined as a filamental pinch in plasma physics, were replicated.

Later terella tests were carried out by a variety of scientists to investigate various features of the Earth's magnetic field in space. According to reports, such trials are difficult to interpret, which is why computer models have mostly supplanted them.

Many other observations of significant electrical activity on the sun's surface and in the solar wind have been made. Scientists have discovered "jet streams" or "rivers" of hot electrically charged gas flowing beneath the surface of the Sun using the Solar and Heliospheric Observatory (SOHO) spacecraft.

The space plasma physics community is working to extend plasma physics understanding to the Sun and other astrophysical objects. The National Aeronautics and Space Administration's (NASA) panel on Sun-Solar System Connection 2005–2035, which was dedicated to that goal, identified four fundamental processes as the critical immediate steps: magnetic reconnection, particle acceleration, plasma and neutral interactions physics, and the generation and variability of magnetic fields with their coupling to structures throughout the heliosphere.

The ubiquitous themes of energy conversion and transport, cross-scale interaction, turbulence, and nonlinear physics—concepts that are crucial to the understanding of space and planetary systems—are present in each of these research focus areas. Understanding the causes and effects of solar variability, as well as the Sun's influence on the Earth's atmosphere and geospace, is a scientific endeavour motivated by both intellectual curiosity and societal requirements. Understanding the fundamental physics of plasma is required for the Sun–Solar System Connection.

Space weather

The solar wind and the interplanetary magnetic field (IMF) carried by the solar wind plasma influence space weather within the Solar System. Geomagnetic storms and substorms, energization of the Van Allen radiation belts, ionospheric disturbances and scintillation of satellite-to-ground radio transmissions and long-range radar signals, aurora, and geomagnetically produced currents near Earth's surface are all examples of space weather. CMEs (coronal mass ejections) are major space weather drivers because they can compress the magnetosphere and cause geomagnetic storms.

Solar energetic particles (SEP) driven by coronal mass ejections or solar flares can cause solar particle events (SPEs), which can destroy equipment onboard spacecraft e.g. Galaxy 15 failure, endanger astronauts‘ lives, and enhance radiation hazards to high-altitude, high-latitude aviation.As the space era began and satellites began to measure the space environment, the phrase "space weather" was coined in the late 1950s. The phrase resurfaced in the 1990s, accompanied by the conviction that the impact of space on human systems necessitated a more coordinated study and application framework.

Solar energetic particles (SEP) driven by coronal mass ejections

As military and commercial systems became more reliant on space weather in the twentieth century, and as a result interest in space weather grew. Satellite communications are an important aspect of global commerce. Satellite weather systems offer data on the weather on the ground. Signals from the Global Positioning System (GPS) satellites are used in a wide range of applications. Space weather can interfere with or damage these satellites, as well as the radio signals they use to communicate.

The exposure of a human body to radiation in space has the harmful effects. The ever-present radiationbelts extend down to the altitude of crewed spacecraft such as the International Space Station (ISS) and the Space Shuttle, but the amount of exposure is within the acceptable lifetime exposure limit under normal conditions. During a major space weather event that includes an Solar energetic particles (SEP) burst from sun, the flux can increase by orders of magnitude. Areas within ISS provide shielding that can keep the total dose within safe limits. For the Space Shuttle, such an event would have required immediate mission termination.

Space weather observation is carried out for both scientific and practical purposes. Scientific observation has progressed in tandem with advances in knowledge, whereas application-related observation has grown in tandem with the ability to harness such data.

At ground level, space weather is monitored by analyzing variations in the Earth's magnetic field across timescales ranging from seconds to days, as well as the surface of the Sun and radio noise created in the Sun's atmosphere.

Ground-based magnetometers and magnetic observatories provide essential space weather monitoring data. Magnetic storms were initially identified by measuring magnetic disturbances on the ground. Data from ground magnetometers provide situational awareness in real time for post-event study. Magnetic observatories have been in operation for decades to centuries, collecting data to help researchers better understand long-term changes in space climatology.

The photosphere of the Sun is constantly monitored for activity that could lead to solar flares and CMEs. The Global Oscillation Network Group (GONG) project uses helioseismology, the study of sound waves propagating through the Sun and detected as ripples on the solar surface, to monitor both the surface and the inside of the Sun. On the far side of the Sun, GONG can detect sunspot groups. Visual observations from the STEREO spacecraft have confirmed this capacity.

Cosmic rays from the Sun and other galactic sources are monitored indirectly by neutron detectors on the ground.

When cosmic rays collide with the atmosphere, atomic interactions occur, resulting in a shower of lower-energy particles falling into the atmosphere and eventually reaching earth level. Monitoring high-energy neutrons at ground level can detect the existence of cosmic rays in the near-Earth space environment. Small fluxes of cosmic rays are always present. During situations involving energetic solar flares, the Sun produces large fluxes.

The strength with which space weather magnetic fields, such as coronal mass ejections, couple with the Earth's magnetic field is referred to as geoeffectiveness. The direction of the magnetic field contained within the plasma that comes from the Sun determines this. To determine field direction, new approaches for measuring Faraday Rotation in radio waves are being developed.

Space weather has been studied by a number of research missions. The Orbiting Geophysical Observatory series was one of the earliest spacecraft to study the environment in orbit. The NASA-ESA Solar-Terrestrial Relations Observatory (STEREO) pair of spacecraft was launched into solar orbit in 2006, while the Van Allen Probes were launched into a very elliptical Earth orbit in 2012.

Monitoring the Sun, in addition to the solar wind, is critical for space weather. Because the solar EUV cannot be monitored from the ground, the joint NASA-ESA Solar and Heliospheric Observatory (SOHO) satellite was launched and has given solar EUV photos beginning in 1995. SOHO, which inspired the STEREO mission, is a major source of near-real-time solar data for both science and space weather prediction.

The Deep Space Climate Observatory (DSCOVR) satellite was launched in February 2015 by NOAA as an Earth observation and space weather satellite. One of its features is the ability to predict coronal mass ejections in advance.

During the first decade of the twenty-first century, a commercial space weather sector arose, servicing the governmental, academic, commercial, and consumer sectors. Smaller firms or divisions inside bigger companies that supply space weather data, models, derivative products, and service distribution are often known as space weather providers.

Researchers in science and engineering, as well as users, make up the commercial sector. The focus of the activities is on the effects of space weather on technology. The American Commercial Space Weather Association (ACSWA) was founded on April 29, 2010 by the commercial space weather sector. For national infrastructure, economic strength, and national security, ACSWA advocates space weather risk reduction.

Plasma astrophysics

Astrophysical plasma is plasma outside of the Solar System. Space plasma, which includes the plasma of the Sun, the solar wind, and the ionospheres and magnetospheres of the Earth and other planets, is often distinguished from astrophysical plasma.It is often spotted in space and is investigated as part of astrophysics. Many physicists believe that this is the state in which much of the universe's baryonic matter exists.

Matter becomes ionised and becomes plasma when it becomes sufficiently hot and energetic. Negatively-charged electrons and positively-charged ions are among the constituent particles of matter broken down by this process. Local electromagnetic fields can have an impact on these electrically charged particles. This comprises star-generated strong fields as well as weak fields seen in star-forming regions, interstellar space, and intergalactic space. Electric fields are also seen in some star astrophysical phenomena, but they are insignificant in low-density gaseous mediums.

The Plasma Astrophysics helps to understand some of the most fascinating and important astrophysical phenomena, such as:

- Pulsar magnetospheres and pulsar wind nebulae (PWN)
- Blazar/AGN jets
- Gamma-ray bursts (GRBs)
- Coronae of accreting black holes in AGN and XRBs
- Turbulent accretion disks around black holes and their magnetically-active coronae.
- Magnetic reconnection in high-energy-density astrophysical plasmas with applications to magnetar flares and gamma-ray bursts.
- Quantum plasma physics

Gamma-ray bursts

Because they generate electromagnetic radiation across a wide range of the electromagnetic spectrum, astrophysical plasma can be examined in a variety of ways. Because astrophysical plasmas are often hot, electrons in them release X-rays all the time through a process known as bremsstrahlung. X-ray telescopes in the high atmosphere or in space may be used to detect this radiation. Radio waves and gamma rays are also emitted by astrophysical plasmas.

Star plasmas can generate and interact with magnetic fields, resulting in a wide range of dynamic astrophysical phenomena. Due to the Zeeman effect, these phenomena can sometimes be seen in spectra. Preexisting weak magnetic fields can influence other types of astrophysical plasmas, whose interactions can only be determined indirectly using polarimetry or other indirect approaches. Diffuse plasmas are found in the intergalactic medium, interstellar medium, interplanetary medium, and solar winds, among other places.Prior to recombination, the entire cosmos was in a plasma state, according to Big Bang theory. Following the formation of the first quasars, much of the universe reionized.

The study of astrophysical plasmas is a standard aspect of academic astrophysics. Despite the fact that plasma processes are included in the traditional cosmological model, recent theories suggest that they may only play a minimal role in the formation of the very biggest structures, such as voids, galaxy clusters, and superclusters.In tight binary star systems, astrophysical plasmas can be found in accretion discs around stars or compact objects like white dwarfs, neutron stars, or black holes. Plasma is linked to material ejection in astrophysical jets, such as those seen with accreting black holes or in active galaxies such as M87's jet, which may reach out to 5,000 light-years.Plasmas are by far the most common phase of ordinary matter in the universe, both by mass and by volume.

Plasma Astrophysics strives to learn more about how plasmas behave in order to better comprehend the creation, evolution, and death of the many different structures we can see in the universe, ranging from stars and planetary systems to galaxies and clusters of galaxies.

Relativistic Astrophysics

The area of astrophysics that investigates astronomical events and celestial bodies for which classical mechanics and Newton's law of gravitation are inapplicable is known as relativistic astrophysics. A century after the inception of general relativity theory, the discipline of relativistic astrophysics began with Schwarzschild's solution and continues to grow at a breakneck pace.

Relativistic astrophysics outlines the relativity theory and lists some situations where this theory is needed: radio galaxies, micro-quasars, gamma rays, cosmic rays, neutron stars, x-ray sources, the solar system, and the universe.Astrophysical relativity is a method for determining the features of large-scale objects in which gravitation plays a substantial part in the physical phenomena studied, as well as the foundation for black hole (astro)physics and gravitational wave research.

Gravitational wave

Gravitational waves are ripples in the curvature of spacetime caused by accelerating masses that propagate as waves at the speed of light outward from their source. They were first hypothesised by Oliver Heaviside in 1893, followed by Henri Poincaré in 1905, and then Albert Einstein predicted them in 1916 using his general theory of relativity.

Compact binaries-source of Gravitational waves

Observations of gravity waves are utilised in gravitational-wave astronomy to deduce information about the origins of gravitational waves. Binary star systems made up of white dwarfs, neutron stars, and black holes, as well as supernovae and the development of the early cosmos immediately after the Big Bang, are examples of sources that can be investigated this manner.Many systems can release gravitational waves, but the source must consist of extremely big particles moving at a considerable fraction of the speed of light to produce detectable signals. A binary of two compact items serves as the primary source.

The following are some examples of systems:

- Compact binaries made up of two closely orbiting stellar-mass objects, such as white dwarfs, neutron stars or black holes.
- Supermassive black hole binaries-These are potentially the loudest gravitational-wave signals.
- Extreme-mass-ratio systems of a stellar-mass compact object orbiting a supermassive black hole.

In addition to binaries, there are other potential sources:

- Supernovae generate high-frequency bursts of gravitational waves that could be detected with LIGO or Virgo.
- Rotating neutron stars are a source of continuous high-frequency waves if they possess axial asymmetry.
- Early universe processes, such as inflation or a phase transition.
- Cosmic strings could also emit gravitational radiation if they do exist. Discovery of these gravitational waves would confirm the existence of cosmic strings.

Gravitational waves can also be utilised to observe systems that would otherwise be invisible or nearly difficult to detect. They, for example, offer a one-of-a-kind method of determining the properties of black holes.

Gravity is presented as a phenomena originating from the curvature of spacetime in Einstein's general theory of relativity. The existence of mass causes this curvature. The larger the mass contained within a particular volume of space, the greater the curvature of spacetime at the volume's volume's boundary.

The curvature of spacetime changes as things with mass move around in it, reflecting the changes in their locations. Accelerating objects cause changes in this curvature to spread outwards at the speed of light in a wave-like way in certain conditions. These propagating phenomena are known as gravitational waves.

Gravitational waves might theoretically occur at any frequency. Very low frequency waves, on the other hand, would be impossible to detect, and there is no reliable source for detectable very high frequency waves.During their in-spiral, merger, and ring-down phases, black hole binaries generate gravitational waves. During the merging phase, the maximum amplitude of emission occurs, which may be modelled using numerical relativity techniques. The merger of two black holes produced the first direct observation of gravitational waves.

A supernova is a fleeting astronomical event that occurs during the late stellar developmental phases of the life of a giant star, and is characterised by a dramatic and cataclysmic explosion. This explosion can occur in a variety of ways, but in all of them, a major percentage of the mass in the star is pushed out into the surrounding space at extremely high speeds, up to 10% the speed of light.

There will be gravitational radiation from these explosions unless they have complete spherical symmetry i.e., stuff is spewed out evenly in all directions. This is due to the fact that gravitational waves are caused by a changing quadrupole moment, which can only occur when masses move asymmetrically.

Gravitational waves possess two distinct characteristics. For starters, no matter has to be nearby for waves to be generated by a binary system of uncharged black holes that release no electromagnetic radiation. Second, gravitational waves can pass through any stuff in their path without being appreciably scattered. Whereas interstellar dust, for example, might block light from distant stars, gravitational waves will pass through practically unhindered. These two characteristics enable gravitational waves to carry data about cosmic phenomena that humans have never seen before.

Gravitational waves are constantly passing Earth; however, even the strongest have a minuscule effect and their sources are generally at a great distance.Improved detectors became operational in 2015 after years of producing null data.

The LIGO-Virgo collaborations announced the first detection of gravitational waves on February 11, 2016, based on a signal (named GW150914) observed on September 14, 2015, from two black holes with masses of 29 and 36 solar masses merging some 1.3 billion light-years away. The new merging black hole has a mass of 62 solar masses.

Gravitational waves emitted energy equivalent to three solar masses. Both LIGO detectors in Livingston and Hanford picked up the signal. The signal came from the Southern Celestial Hemisphere, roughly in the direction of the Magellanic Clouds although considerably farther away. The probability of this being a gravitational wave observation was 99.99994 percent.

Electromagnetic waves cannot reach some portions of space, but gravitational waves can. They enable the study of black hole mergers and maybe other strange objects in the furthest reaches of the Universe. Gravitational wave astronomy provides novel insights into the workings of the Universe that cannot be studied using more traditional methods such as optical observatories or radio telescopes.

Gravitational waves, in particular, could be of interest to cosmologists since they provide a chance to see the very early Universe.

Gravitational-wave observations complement electromagnetic-spectrum observations. These waves also have the potential to provide information in ways that are not possible to obtain through the detection and analysis of electromagnetic waves.

Electromagnetic waves can be absorbed and re-radiated in a variety of ways, making it difficult to retrieve information about the source.

Gravitational waves, on the other hand, only have a weak interaction with matter, therefore they are not scattered or absorbed. Astronomers should be able to see the centre of a supernova, star nebulae, and perhaps merging galactic cores in unprecedented ways as a result of this.

Gravitational-wave astronomy is still in its infancy as a field of study; nonetheless, the astrophysics community agrees that it will develop into a well-established component of 21st-century multi-messenger astronomy.

Gravitational lensing

A gravitational lens is a collection of mass between a distant light source and an observer, such as a cluster of galaxies, that can bend light from the source as it travels toward the observer. Gravitational lensing is the name for this phenomenon, and the degree of bending is one of Albert Einstein's general theory of relativity's predictions.

Gravitational lens

Henry Cavendish in an unpublished manuscript in 1784 and Johann Georg von Soldner's paper published in 1804 both pointed out that Newtonian gravity predicts that starlight will bend around a big object, as Isaac Newton predicted in his book Opticks in 1704. Einstein obtained the same result as Soldner in 1911 using only the equivalence principle. However, while finishing general relativity in 1915, Einstein discovered that his and hence Soldner's 1911-result is just half of the right value. Einstein was the first to compute the proper light bending value.

The first observation of light deflection was made by observing the position of stars on the celestial sphere as they travelled near the Sun. During the total solar eclipse on May 29, 1919, Arthur Eddington, Frank Watson Dyson, and their partners made the observations. The solar eclipse allowed people to see the stars close to the Sun. Observations were made in Sobral, Ceará, Brazil, and So Tomé and Prncipe, on the west coast of Africa, at the same time. The observations revealed that light from stars passing close to the Sun was slightly bent, causing stars to appear out of place.

Gravitational lensing has evolved into a well-established discipline of astrophysics and a potent instrument for addressing significant cosmological challenges in the quarter-century after its discovery. The Gravitational lensing is used in studies of galactic and subgalactic sizes phenomena, where other methods such as cosmic microwave background variations or statistical features of the universe's large scale structure provide little insight.Gravitational lensing probes the distribution of matter in galaxies and clusters of galaxies, and enables observations of the distant universe.

Applications include:

- Direct detection and characterization of the properties of dark matter.
- Use of lenses as gravitational telescopes to identify the most distant galaxies and the sources of cosmic hydrogen reionization beyond redshift seven.
- Study of supermassive black-holes at cosmological distances.

A point-like gravitational lens, unlike an optical lens, produces a maximum deflection of light passing closest to its centre and a minimum deflection of light passing farthest from its centre. As a result, a gravitational lens has a focal line rather than a single focal point. O.J. Lodge coined the term "lens" to describe gravitational light deflection, stating that "it is not admissible to argue that the solar gravitational field behaves like a lens, because it has no focal length." The original light source will appear as a ring around the enormous lensing object if the source, the massive lensing object, and the observer are all in a straight line.

The quantity and shape of distorted images of the same source seen by the observer depends on the relative positions of the source, lens, and observer, as well as the shape of the lensing object's gravitational well of the lensing object.

Gravitational lensing is divided into three categories.

Strong lensing

Strong gravitational lensing is a gravitational lensing effect that is strong enough to produce multiple images, arcs, or even Einstein rings.Even a galaxy with a mass 100 billion times that of the Sun will create several pictures spaced by only a few arcseconds, despite being termed "strong." The spacing between galaxy clusters can be many arcminutes. The galaxies and sources in both cases are hundreds of millions of light years away from our Galaxy.

Weak lensing

While any mass bends the path of light passing near it, it rarely creates the massive arcs and multiple pictures associated with severe gravitational lensing. The weak lensing regime encompasses the vast majority of lines of sight in the cosmos, where deflection is impossible to detect in a single background source.Weak gravitational lensing is essentially a statistical measurement, but it allows scientists to determine the masses of celestial objects without having to make assumptions about their composition or dynamical state.

It is possible to quantify the shear of the lensing field in any region by averaging the shapes and orientations of a large number of distant galaxies. This can then be used to recreate the mass distribution in the area, including the dark matter background distribution. Because galaxies are intrinsically elliptical and the weak gravitational lensing signal is modest, these surveys must use a large number of galaxies.

Gravitational microlensing

Gravitational microlensing, an astronomical phenomena can identify objects with masses ranging from a planet's mass to a star's mass, independent of the light they emit. Astronomers can typically discover only brilliant objects that emit a lot of light or big objects that block background light clouds of gas and dust. These objects make up a small part of a galaxy's mass. Microlensing allows researchers to investigate things that emit very little or no light.

When a distant star or quasar is sufficiently aligned with a massive compact foreground object, the bending of light due to its gravitational field produces two distorted images,resulting in an observable magnification, as discussed by Albert Einstein in 1915. The foreground item's mass, as well as the relative proper motion between the background'source' and the foreground 'lens' object, determine the transient brightening's time scale.

Microlensing that is perfectly aligned creates a clear buffer between the lens's radiation and the source objects. It enlarges or reveals the distant source, increasing its size and/or brightness.Brown dwarfs, red dwarfs, planets, white dwarfs, neutron stars, black holes, and huge compact halo objects can all be studied using this technique. Such lensing magnifies and produces a wide range of conceivable warping for distant source objects emitting any type of electromagnetic radiation at all wavelengths.

Planets outside our solar system have been discovered using microlensing techniques. Most stars in the Milky Way galaxy had at least one orbiting planet, according to a statistical analysis of individual examples of detected microlensing from 2002 to 2007.

Most gravitational lenses have been discovered by chance in the past. The finding of 22 new gravitational lensing systems in the northern hemisphere (Cosmic Lens All Sky Survey, CLASS), which was conducted in radio frequencies utilising the Very Large Array (VLA) in New Mexico, was a major milestone. This has opened up a whole new field of research, from locating very far away objects to determining values for cosmological parameters so we may better understand the cosmos.

Physical cosmology

Physical cosmology is a subfield of cosmology that studies cosmological models. A cosmological model, or simply cosmology, describes the universe's largest-scale structures and processes, allowing basic questions concerning the universe's origin, structure, evolution, and ultimate fate to be studied.

Cosmology is greatly influenced by the study of many different areas of theoretical and applied physics. Particle physics experiments and theory, theoretical and observational astrophysics, general relativity, quantum mechanics, and plasma physics are all crucial to cosmology.

Cosmology is concerned with the history of the cosmos.Through scientific observation and experiment, physics and astrophysics have played a critical role in defining our understanding of the cosmos. Physical cosmology was shaped by both mathematics and observation in an investigation of the whole universe.

The Big Bang is assumed to have started the universe, followed almost instantly by cosmic inflation, a space expansion from which the universe is thought to have formed 13.799 0.021 billion years ago.Cosmogony examines the origin of the Universe, while cosmography records its properties.

Physical cosmology as we know it today began with Albert Einstein's general theory of relativity, which was developed in 1915, and was followed by major observational discoveries in the 1920s: first, Edwin Hubble discovered that the universe contains a large number of external galaxies beyond the Milky Way, and then work by Vesto Slipher and others demonstrated that the universe is expanding.

These advancements allowed scientists to theorise about the birth of the universe, and Georges Lemaître's Big Bang idea became the prevailing cosmological model.

According to the major forces and processes in each age, the history of the cosmos is divided into different periods termed epochs. The Lambda-CDM model is the standard cosmological model.

The cosmological principle and the dominant role of gravitation are two fundamental premises of current universe models. The two main theories are the big-bang hypothesis and the steady-state hypothesis, with many variations on each basic approach.

Big Bang theory :After Hubble's proof of the continually expanding cosmos in 1929 and especially after Arno Penzias and Robert Wilson's discovery of cosmic microwave background radiation in 1965, some variation of the Big Bang theory has become the dominant scientific view. According to the hypothesis, the universe began between 13 and 14 billion years ago in an infinitely small, endlessly dense point or singularity, from which it has been expanding ever since.

Steady state theory :Since the Big Bang theory was widely accepted by the scientific community, this non-standard cosmology i.e., one that is contrary to the conventional Big Bang model has appeared in numerous forms. In 1948, English scientist Fred Hoyle and Austrians Thomas Gold and Hermann Bondi suggested a popular form of the steady state cosmos. It anticipated a cosmos that expanded but didn't change density, with matter introduced into the universe as it expanded to keep the density constant.

A number of other cosmological theories satisfy both the cosmological principle and general relativity.

Inflationary (or Inflating) Universe - In 1980, American physicist Alan Guth proposed a model of the universe based on the Big Bang but incorporating a brief, early period of exponential cosmic inflation to solve the standard Big Bang model's horizon and flatness problems. The cyclic model, which features an inflationary universe expanding and contracting in cycles and was devised by Paul Steinhardt and Neil Turok in 2002 utilising state-of-the-art M-theory, superstring theory, and brane cosmology, is another form of the inflationary world.

Multiverse Theory-Andrei Linde, a Russian-American physicist, expanded on the inflationary universe concept in 1983 with his chaotic inflation theory or everlasting inflation, which views our universe as one of many "bubbles" that grew as part of a multiverse due to a vacuum that had not decayed to its ground state. Hugh Everett III and Bryce DeWitt, two American physicists, devised and popularised their "many worlds" multiverse formulation in the 1960s and 1970s.

Alternative interpretations have been proposed in which our observable universe is simply one small organised component of an endlessly huge cosmos that is essentially chaotic, or in which our ordered universe is merely one transient episode in an infinite series of largely chaotic and unorganised structures.

One of the most significant tasks in cosmology is to understand the genesis and evolution of the largest and earliest structures, such as quasars, galaxies, clusters, and superclusters. Cosmologists investigate a model of hierarchical structure creation in which smaller items originate initially while larger objects, such as superclusters, are still forming.

Surveying visible galaxies in order to generate a three-dimensional picture of the universe's galaxies and measure the matter power spectrum is one technique to examine structure in the universe. The Sloan Digital Sky Survey and the 2dF Galaxy Redshift Survey both take this strategy.

Simulations, which cosmologists employ to examine the gravitational aggregation of matter in the universe as it clusters into filaments, superclusters, and voids, are another method for understanding structure development. Because there is significantly more dark matter in the universe than visible baryonic matter,most simulations only feature non-baryonic cold dark matter, which should serve to explain the cosmos on the biggest scales.

Simulations that include baryons and examine the creation of individual galaxies are becoming more advanced. Cosmologists examine these simulations to determine if they agree with galaxy surveys and to figure out why there is a difference.

Cosmologists also study:

- Whether primordial black holes were formed in our universe, and what happened to them.
- Detection of cosmic rays and whether it signals a failure of special relativity at high energies.
- The equivalence principle, whether or not Einstein's general theory of relativity is the correct theory of gravitation,and if the fundamental laws of physics are the same everywhere in the universe

There are around 100 billion galaxies in the visible cosmos which aren't just strewn.Gravity has gathered them into a massive cosmic web known as the universe's large-scale structure. On a larger scale, galaxies contain signs of sound waves known as baryon acoustic oscillations (BAO) that swept throughout the cosmos prior to the formation of the cosmic microwave background (CMB). Cosmologists examine large-scale structure and BAO in order to determine the pace of cosmic expansion and comprehend how galaxies are arranged on the biggest sizes.

The atoms that make up the universe only make up around 5% of its total mass. Dark matter and dark energy make up the rest. Dark matter, which makes up about a quarter of the universe's mass, provides the gravitational foundation for the formation of galaxies and galaxy clusters. Dark matter is responsible for the universe's large-scale structure, but we still don't know what it's made of.

The remaining 68 percent of the universe's contents, dark energy, causes the universe's expansion to speed up.Because the push-pull of dark matter and energy is what gives the cosmos its appearance, it is a major subject in contemporary cosmology to figure out exactly what these mystery components are and how they work.

Since the 1990s, dramatic advancements in observational cosmology have led to the establishment of a standard model of cosmology, encompassing the cosmic microwave background, distant supernovae, and galaxy redshift surveys. The model assumes that the universe contains significant amounts of dark matter and dark energy, the nature of which is currently unknown, but the model provides specific predictions that are in excellent accord with a wide range of observations.

PLANETARY SCIENCE

CHAPTER THREE

PLANETARY SCIENCE

Planetary Astronomy

Planetary Astronomy is a science that is both observational and theoretical. Planetary Astronomy, sometimes known as planetology, is the study of planets including Earth, moons, and planetary systems particularly those of the Solar System, as well as the processes that shape them

Observational researchers are primarily interested in the study of the **Small Solar System body (SSSB)** that is neither a planet, a dwarf planet, nor a natural satellite and those that are observed by telescopes, both optical and radio, in order to determine characteristics such as shape, spin, surface materials, and weathering, as well as the history of their formation and evolution.

Space exploration, primarily with robotic spacecraft missions using remote sensing, and comparative, experimental work in Earth-based laboratories can all be part of observational research.

The application of celestial mechanics- a branch of physics that produces ephemeris data by applying physics concepts classical mechanics to astronomical objects like stars and planets and extra solar planetary systems is the focus of theoretical planetary astronomy. The theoretical component involves considerable computer simulation and mathematical modelling.

Planetary Astronomy studies the planetary system also referred to as exoplanetary systems which is a collection of non-stellar objects in or out of orbit around a star or star system that are gravitationally bonded. A planetary system is defined as a system with one or more planets, though it can also include things like as dwarf planets, asteroids, natural satellites, meteoroids, comets, planetesimals, and circumstellar discs.

The finding of numerous terrestrial-mass planets circling the pulsar PSR B1257+12 in 1992 was the first confirmed detection of an exoplanet. In 1995, a large planet called 51 Pegasi b was discovered in a four-day orbit around the neighbouring G-type star 51 Pegasi, marking the first verified identification of exoplanets from a main-sequence star. Since then, the number of detections has risen, thanks to improvements in methods for detecting extrasolar planets and dedicated planet-finding programmes like the Kepler mission.

NASA launched the Kepler space telescope to search for planets the size of Earth orbiting other stars. The spacecraft, named for astronomer Johannes Kepler, was launched into an Earth-trailing heliocentric orbit on March 7, 2009.

Kepler's sole scientific instrument was a photometer that continuously monitored the brightness of approximately 150,000 main sequence stars in a fixed field of view. It was designed to survey a portion of Earth's region of the Milky Way in order to discover Earth-size exoplanets in or near habitable zones and estimate how many of the Milky Way's billions of stars have such planets.

The Milky Way spans 100,000 light-years vast, yet as of July 2014, 90% of planets with known distances are within 2000 light-years of Earth. Micro lensing is one method for detecting planets that are much further away. The gravitational lens effect causes gravitational micro lensing, which is an astronomical phenomenon. It can identify objects with masses ranging from a planet's mass to a star's mass, independent of the light they emit.

Based on data from the Kepler satellite mission, astronomers estimated that there could be up to 40 billion Earth- and super-Earth-sized planets orbiting in the habitable zones of Sun-like stars and red dwarfs in the Milky Way in 2013. It's possible that 11 billion of these planets are orbiting Sun-like stars. According to the researchers, the closest such planet may be 12 light-years away. However, because planets as tiny as Earth have been discovered to be gas planets, this does not provide estimates for the number of extrasolar terrestrial planets.

Formations of Planetary systems

Proto planetary discs grow around stars as part of the star formation process, and these discs give rise to planetary systems. Much material is gravitationally distributed into far orbits during the creation of a system, and some planets are ejected totally from the system, becoming rogue planets.

Proto planetary disc around stars

If an evolved star is part of a binary or multiple system, the mass it loses can be transferred to another star, generating new proto planetary discs and second- and third-generation planets that may have different compositions than the initial planets and may be altered by the mass transfer.

There have been discoveries of planets around pulsars. Pulsars are the leftovers of high-mass star supernova explosions, but any planetary system that existed before the supernova would almost certainly be obliterated. Planets would either evaporate, be pushed off their orbits by the exploding star's gas, or escape the gravitational hold of the central star due to the sudden loss of most of the star's mass, or, in some cases, the supernova would kick the pulsar out of the system at high velocity, leaving any planets that had survived the explosion as free-floating objects.

Planets discovered near pulsars could have developed as a result of pre-existing star partners that were nearly completely vaporised by the supernova blast, leaving behind planet-sized bodies. Planets could also develop in an accretion disc of falling matter that surrounds a pulsar. Matter-fallback discs that failed to leave orbit following a supernova could create planets surrounding black holes.

Stars consume the inner planets as they expand into red giants, asymptotic giant branch stars, and planetary nebulae, evaporating or partially evaporating them depending on their mass. Planets that are not consumed travel further away from the star as it loses mass.

The majority of known exoplanets orbit stars that are spectrally similar to the Sun: main-sequence stars in the spectral categories F, G, or K. One explanation for this is that planet-hunting programmes have a tendency to focus on such stars. Furthermore, statistical analyses show that lower-mass stars red dwarfs with spectral category M are less likely to host planets large enough to be identified using the radial-velocity method. Despite this, the Kepler spacecraft has detected tens of planets orbiting red dwarfs using the transit method, which can detect tiny planets.

Diverse galaxies have varied histories of star creation and, as a result, different histories of planet formation. Planet formation is affected by the ages, metallicities, and orbits of star populations within a galaxy. The distribution of star populations within a galaxy changes depending on the galaxy type.

In comparison to spiral galaxies, stars in elliptical galaxies are substantially older. The majority of elliptical galaxies have low-mass stars and little star formation activity. The distribution of different forms of galaxies in the cosmos is determined by their location inside galaxy clusters, with elliptical galaxies being located near the cluster's centre.

The habitable zone around a star is the temperature range in which liquid water can exist on a planet without evaporating or freezing; that is, not too close to the star for the water to evaporate and not too far away for the water to freeze. Because the amount of heat produced by stars varies based on their size and age, the habitable zone will likewise change. The planet's ability to hold heat is also influenced by its atmospheric conditions, hence the location of the habitable zone is unique to each type of planet.

The Venus zone is the area surrounding a star where a terrestrial planet would experience runaway greenhouse conditions similar to Venus, but not so close to the star that its atmosphere would totally evaporate. The position of the Venus zone, like the habitable zone, is determined by various factors, including the kind of star and planet parameters such as mass, rotation rate, and atmospheric clouds. Based on planet size and distance from star, studies of the Kepler satellite data show that 32 percent of red dwarfs have possibly Venus-like planets.

Planetary geology

Planetary geology includes such topics as determining the internal structure of the terrestrial planets, and also looks at planetary volcanism and surface processes such as impact craters, fluvial and aeolianprocesses. The structures and compositions of the giant planets and their moons are also examined, as is the make-up of the minor bodies of the Solar System, such as asteroids, the Kuiper Belt, and comets.

Astrogeology, sometimes known as exogeology, is a branch of planetary science that studies the geology of celestial bodies such planets and their moons, asteroids, comets, and meteorites.

Eugene Shoemaker is credited with applying geologic ideas to planetary mapping and founding the Astrogeology Research Program inside the United States Geological Survey in the early 1960s. He made significant contributions to the field of impact craters, Selenography (Moon studies), asteroids, and comets.

The most well-known planetary geology research topics are the Moon and the two neighbouring planets, Venus and Mars, which are all in close proximity to the Earth. The Moon was investigated first, utilising techniques used earlier on Earth.

Geomorphology investigates planetary surface features and reconstructs their creation history by inferring the physical processes that acted on the surface.The geology of solar terrestrial planets is primarily concerned with the geological properties of the Solar System's four terrestrial planets - Mercury, Venus, Earth, and Mars – as well as one terrestrial dwarf planet, Ceres.

Terrestrial planets differ significantly from gigantic planets, which may or may not have solid surfaces and are mostly made up of a mixture of hydrogen, helium, and water in various physical states. The stony surfaces of terrestrial planets are compact, and Venus, Earth, and Mars all have atmospheres. The terrestrial planets all have a similar structure: a central metallic core, primarily iron, with a silicate mantle surrounding them. Three of the four solar terrestrial planets Venus, Earth, and Mars have atmospheres, and all include impact craters and tectonic characteristics like rift valleys and volcanoes.

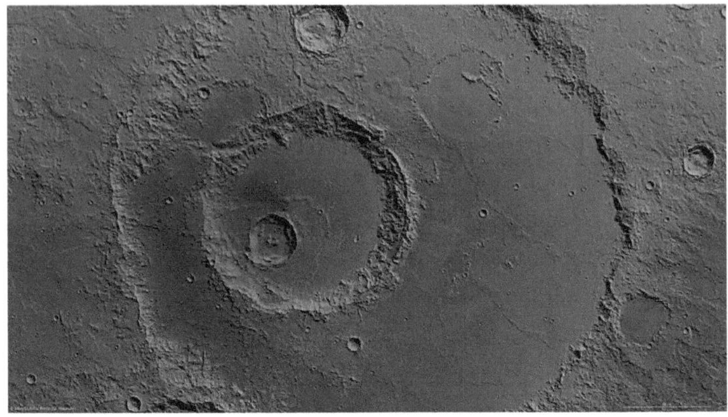

Hadley Crater in Mars

Giant planets are a diverse group of planets that are significantly larger than Earth. They're usually made up of low-boiling-point elements gases or ices rather than rock or other solid things, but enormous solid planets can exist as well. Jupiter, Saturn, Uranus, and Neptune are the four known big planets in the Solar System. There have been numerous extrasolar massive planets discovered orbiting other stars.

The majority of planets discovered outside the Solar System are large planets, which are easier to detect. Hundreds of potentially terrestrial extra solar planets have been discovered since 2005, with some confirmed as terrestrial. The majority of them are super-Earths, or planets with masses between Earth's and Neptune's; depending on their mass and other criteria, super-Earths can be gas planets or terrestrial planets.

Planetary surface geology

Surface geology is a branch of planetary geology that studies planetary surfaces. A planetary surface is the point where the solid or liquid substance of an astronomical object's outer crust meets the atmosphere or outer space. Terrestrial planets including Earth, dwarf planets, natural satellites, planetesimals, and many other tiny Solar System entities have planetary surfaces (SSSBs).

From the inner terrestrial planets to the asteroid belt, natural satellites of gas giant planets, and beyond to the Trans-Neptunian objects, planetary surfaces can be found all around the Solar System. Surface conditions, temperatures, and terrain change dramatically due to a variety of factors,which is often produced by the surfaces themselves. Surface area, surface gravity, surface temperature, and surface pressure are all measurements of surface conditions. Aeolian processes, hydrology, subduction, volcanism, sediment, and seismic activity can all affect surface stability. Some surfaces vary over time, while others stay the same for millions of years.

Water ice appears to be the most frequent planetary surface substance in the Solar System. Surface ice can be found as close to the Sun as Mercury, but it is more plentiful beyond Mars. Solid matter in the form of rock, regolith, and frozen chemical elements and chemical compounds are examples of other surfaces. Beyond the frost line, ice predominates on planetary surfaces, whereas rock and regolith predominate closer to the Sun. Minerals and hydrates may also be found in trace amounts on many planetary surfaces.

Gas giants are usually thought to lack a surface, despite the fact that they may contain a solid core of rock or ice, or a liquid core of metallic hydrogen. However, if the planet's core exists, it does not have enough mass to be deemed a surface.A gas giant is a massive planet that is mostly made up of hydrogen and helium. Because they contain the same core ingredients as stars, gas giants are often known as failed stars. The Solar System's gas giants are Jupiter and Saturn.

Surface of Gas gaint Jupiter

While surface liquid is abundant on Earth, the largest body of surface liquid is the World Ocean, it is rare elsewhere, with Titan having the largest known hydrocarbon lake system, while surface water, which is abundant on Earth and essential to all known forms of life, is thought to only exist as seasonal flows on warm Martian slopes and in the habitable zones of other planetary systems. Volcanism can result in lava flows on the surface of geologically active bodies the greatest of which being Io's Amirani volcano flow. Many of Earth's Igneous rocks are formed through processes rare elsewhere, such as the presence of volcanic magma and water.

Organic molecules are increasingly being discovered on objects around the Solar System. Because organic compounds are frequently volatile, their persistence as a solid or liquid on a planetary surface is of scientific interest. Organic compounds could indicate either an intrinsic source, such as from the object's interior or residue from larger quantities of organic material preserved over geological timescales, or an extrinsic source, such as from past or recent collisions with other objects. Organic stuff is difficult to detect due to radiation, making detection on atmosphereless objects closer to the Sun particularly difficult.

Gravity, distance, and other weather conditions makes planetary exploration both costly and perilous. Due to severe low or high atmospheric pressure and unknown causes planetary exploration is difficult mission . This necessitates the use of space probes for early surface exploration.

Many probes are fixed which have a restricted study range, and only survive for a short time on extraterrestrial surfaces, although mobility probes, such as rovers, have examined vast surface areas. Sample return missions allow scientists to examine alien surface materials on Earth without sending a crewed mission, although they are only viable for objects with low gravity and atmosphere.

The lunar surface was the first extraterrestrial planetary surface to be surveyed by Luna 2 in 1959. The Apollo programme includes the first moonwalk on July 20, 1969, and the successful return of extraterrestrial surface samples to Earth, making it the first and only human exploration of an extraterrestrial surface.

On December 15, 1970, Venera 7 became the first probe to land on another planet. The first rover on Mars was Mars Pathfinder in 1997, and the Mars Exploration Rover has been researching the surface of the red planet since 2004. Mars 3 "soft landed" and returned data from Mars on August 22, 1972.

NEAR Shoemaker was the first spacecraft to land softly on an asteroid, 433 Eros, in February 2001, and Hayabusa was the first to return samples from 25143 Itokawa on June 13, 2010. On January 14, 2005, Huygens soft-landed and returned data from Titan.Samples obtained by rovers on the ground and spectroscopy from orbiting satellites have indicated the presence of a number of complex organic chemicals on Mars, some of which may constitute biosignatures in the search for life.

Humans are particularly interested in planetary surfaces and surface life since it is their preferred home, having evolved to move over land and breathe air. As a result, human space exploration and colonisation are largely focused on them. Only the surface of the Earth and the Moon have been directly explored by humans. Direct investigation of even near-Earth objects is dangerous and expensive due to the huge distances and complexities of space.

Ring systems of planets

A planetary ring system is a ring system that surrounds a planet. A ring system is a disc or ring made of solid material such as dust and moonlets that orbits an astronomical object and is a common component of satellite systems around big planets.

Thicker planetary rings that surround planets have been proposed to have formed in three ways:

- From material from the protoplanetary disc that was within the planet's Roche limit and thus couldn't coalesce to form moons,
- From debris from a moon disrupted by a large impact
- From debris from a moon disrupted by tidal stresses when it passed within the planet's Roche limit.

As a result of meteoroid interactions with the planet's moons, fainter planetary rings can emerge. The majority of rings were assumed to be unstable and evaporate over millions or billions of years. Ring particles might be silicate or ice dust, depending on their composition. Larger boulders and rocks may be present. The maximum size of a ring particle is determined by the material's specific strength, density, and tidal force at the particle's height.
Small moons orbiting near the inner or outer borders of rings or within gaps in the rings are known as "shepherd" moons.Material that travels closer to the shepherd moon's orbit is either deflected back into the body of the ring, ejected from the system, or accreted onto the moon itself, thanks to the gravitational pull of shepherd moons.

Exoplanets with rings are possible because all of the Solar System's large planets have rings. The equator of the Solar System's gas giants is aligned with the rings of their planets. Tidal forces from the star, on the other hand, would line the planet's outermost rings with its orbital plane around the star for exoplanets that circle near to their star.

Saturn's rings are the largest ring system of any planet in the Solar System, and have thus been known for a long time. When the Voyager 1 probe first viewed Jupiter's ring system in 1979, it was the third to be discovered, and the Galileo spacecraft investigated it more thoroughly in the 1990s. A faint thick torus known as the "halo," a thin, comparatively bright main ring, and two wide, faint "gossamer rings" are its four primary elements. The system is largely made up of dust.

Saturn's rings

The ring system of Uranus is intermediate in complexity between Saturn's enormous system and the simpler systems of Jupiter and Neptune. James L. Elliot, Edward W. Dunham, and Jessica Mink discovered them in 1977. Observations by Voyager 2 and the Hubble Space Telescope between then and 2005 revealed a total of 13 different rings, the majority of which are opaque and only a few kilometres across. They're dark, and they're probably made up of water ice and radiation-processed organics. Aerodynamic drag from Uranus' long exosphere-corona is responsible for the lack of dust.

The system surrounding Neptune is made up of five main rings, the densest of which are analogous to Saturn's low-density regions. They are, however, faint and dusty, and have a structure that is quite similar to Jupiter's. The very dark material that makes up the rings is most likely organics that have been exposed to radiation, similar to Uranus' rings. Dust makes up 20 to 70% of the rings, which is a significant percentage. The rings have been spotted for decades before Voyager 2 confirmed their existence in 1989.

According to reports from March 2008, Saturn's moon Rhea may have its own tenuous ring system, making it the only moon known to have one. A further research released on 2010 found that Cassini satellite imagery of Rhea did not match the predicted features of the rings, implying that the magnetic effects that lead to the ring hypothesis are caused by another source.

Magnetosphere

A magnetosphere is an area of space surrounding an astronomical object in which charged particles are impacted by that object's magnetic field, as defined in astronomy and planetary science. A celestial body with an active internal dynamo creates it.

The magnetic field resembles a magnetic dipole in the space environment near a planetary body. The flow of electrically conductive plasma emitted from the Sun i.e., the solar wind or a nearby star can drastically alter field lines further out.

Exoplanets, pulsars, and even the galaxy have magnetospheres, as do Mercury, Earth, and the big planets of our Solar System. Magnetospheres are electromagnetically dominated regions that surround celestial bodies.

Magnetospheres are created and maintained by many celestial objects. The Sun, Mercury, Jupiter, Saturn, Uranus, Neptune, and Ganymede are all part of the Solar System which has Magnetospheres . Jupiter's magnetosphere, which stretches up to 7,000,000 kilometres across, is the largest in the Solar System.

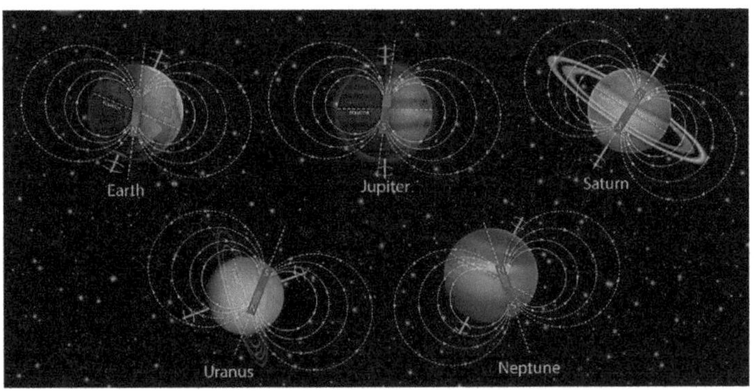

Magnetospheres of Planets

The type of astronomical object, the nature of plasma and momentum sources, the period of the object's spin, the nature of the axis about which the object spins, the axis of the magnetic dipole, and the quantity and direction of solar wind flow are all factors that influence magnetospheres.

The magnetosphere was first studied around 1600, when William Gilbert observed that the magnetic field on Earth's surface matched that of a terrella, a small magnetised sphere. Walter M. Elsasser proposed the dynamo theory model in the 1940s, which links the Earth's magnetic field to the motion of the iron outer core.

Scientists were able to investigate the fluctuations in Earth's magnetic field as a function of time, latitude, and longitude using magnetometers.

Eugene Parker established the concept of the solar wind in 1958, and Thomas Gold proposed the word "magnetosphere" in 1959 to explain how the solar wind interacted with the Earth's magnetic field. The magnetopause was called after the subsequent Explorer 12 expedition in 1961, which was prompted by Cahill and Amazeen's finding in 1963 of a significant decrease in magnetic field intensity near the noon-time meridian. The magnetotail, or distant magnetic field, was discovered by the International Cometary Explorer in 1983.

Structure of magnetosphere

The bow shock is the magnetosphere's outermost layer and the barrier between it and the surrounding medium. This is the barrier between the stellar wind and the interstellar medium for stars; for planets, the speed of the solar wind slows as it approaches the magnetopause.

The magnetosphere's region between the bow shock and the magnetopause is known as the magnetosheath. It is mostly made up of shocked solar wind, with a minor quantity of plasma from the magnetosphere thrown in for good measure.

The magnetopause is the point in the magnetosphere when the pressures of the planetary magnetic field and the solar wind are equal. It's when the magnetosheath's shocked solar wind collides with the object's magnetic field and plasma from the magnetosphere.

The magnetotail is located opposite the compressed magnetic field, and the magnetosphere extends far beyond the astronomical object. The northern and southern tail lobes are the two lobes that make up the tail. Magnetic field lines in the northern tail lobe face the object, whereas those in the southern tail lobe face away. The tail lobes are nearly empty, with only a few charged particles resisting the solar wind's movement.

Planets with active magnetospheres, such as Earth, can mitigate or deflect the impacts of solar or cosmic radiation, protecting all living beings from potentially harmful and dangerous repercussions.

Current research topics include:

- Magnetospheres of Jupiter and Saturn utilising Pioneer, Voyager, Ulysses, Galileo, Cassini, HST data.
- Planetary magnetic field modelling.
- Magnetosphere/Ionosphere coupling
- Analysis of atmosphere/ionosphere/magnetic environment around Venus
- Focus on Titan environment at Saturn
- Icy satellites such as Enceladus, Dione, Rhea, Thethys and their interaction with Saturn's magnetosphere

Exoplanetology

Extrasolar planets had long been suspected by scientists, philosophers, but there was no means of knowing whether they existed.How abundant they were, or how similar they were to the planets of the Solar System were unknown. Astronomers have refuted several detection claims made in the nineteenth century.

In 1988, scientists assumed they had discovered an exoplanet. The finding of numerous terrestrial-mass planets orbiting the pulsar PSR B1257+12 in 1992 provided the first confirmation of detection. [39] When a huge planet was discovered in a four-day orbit around the neighbouring star 51 Pegasi in 1995, it was the first confirmation of an exoplanet circling a main-sequence star. Although some exoplanets have been directly seen by observatories, the vast majority have been discovered through indirect methods like as the transit and radial-velocity approaches. In February 2018, researchers discovered evidence of planets in a faraway galaxy using the Chandra X-ray Observatory and a planet detection technique called microlensing.

Planets can form anywhere from a few to tens of millions of years after their star forms. Planets in the Solar System can only be seen in their current state, but observations of different planetary systems of diverse ages allow us to see planets during various phases of evolution. The observations span from young proto-planetary discs where planets are still forming to several million year old planetary systems. Planets accrete hydrogen/helium envelopes as they develop in a gaseous protoplanetary disc. Over time, these envelopes cool and contract, and some or all of the hydrogen/helium is lost to space, depending on the mass of the planet.

Kepler-62f, a potentially habitable exoplanet discovered by the Kepler space telescope

On average, each star has at least one planet. The majority of known exoplanets orbit stars that are comparable to our Sun. The Kepler spacecraft has detected tens of planets around red dwarf stars. Some planets circle one member of a binary star system, and other circumbinary planets that orbit both members of the binary star system have been discovered. Few planets in triple star systems and in the quadruple system like Kepler-64 have been discovered.

Methods of detecting extrasolar planets

Two types of detection Methods are used to find extrasolar planets

- Direct imaging
- Indirect methods

Direct imaging -All of the exoplanets that have been directly photographed are huge (far larger than Jupiter) and far from their parent star.When compared to their parent stars, planets are exceedingly dim. It's difficult to see such a dim light source, and the parent star creates a glare that tends to drown it out. To eliminate glare, it is important to filter the light from the parent star while allowing the light from the planet to be detected; this is a big technical problem that necessitates extreme optothermal stability.

Dedicated direct-imaging instruments like the Gemini Planet Imager, VLT-SPHERE, and SCExAO will image dozens of gas giants, although the great majority of known extrasolar planets have only been discovered indirectly.

Indirect method used several techniques like

Transit method-When a planet passes in front of the disc of its parent star, the brightness of the star is reduced by a modest amount. The amount by which the star dims is determined by several factors, including its size and the size of the planet.

Radial velocity or Doppler method-The star moves in its own little orbit around the system's centre of mass as a planet orbiting it. Displacements in the star's spectral lines due to the Doppler effect can be used to identify variations in the star's radial velocity—that is, the speed with which it moves towards or away from Earth.

Transit timing variation (TTV)-When multiple planets are present, each one slightly perturbs the others' orbits. Small variations in the times of transit for one planet can thus indicate the presence of another planet, which itself may or may not transit.

Transit duration variation (TDV)-When a planet orbits multiple stars or if the planet has moons, its transit time can significantly vary per transit and this method is used to successfully confirm many transiting circumbinary planets.

Gravitational microlensing-Microlensing occurs when the gravitational field of a star acts like a lens, magnifying the light of a distant background star. Planets orbiting the lensing star can cause detectable anomalies in the magnification as it varies over time.

Astrometry-Astrometry consists of precisely measuring a star's position in the sky and observing the changes in that position over time. The motion of a star due to the gravitational influence of a planet may be observable and successfully used to investigate the properties of planets found in other ways

Pulsar timing-A pulsar the small, ultradense remnant of a star that has exploded as a supernova emits radio waves extremely regularly as it rotates. If planets orbit the pulsar, they will cause slight anomalies in the timing of its observed radio pulses. The first confirmed discovery of an extrasolar planet was made using this method.

Variable star timing (pulsation frequency)-There are various other types of stars that, like pulsars, have periodic activity. A planet orbiting it can occasionally produce deviations from the periodicity. As of 2013, this approach had discovered few planets.

Reflection/emission modulations-When a planet orbits a star relatively close to it, it collects a large amount of starlight. Due to planets having phases from Earth's viewpoint or planets glowing more from one side than the other due to temperature differences, the amount of light changes as the planet circles around the star and this is used to detect the planets.

Relativistic beaming-The observed flux from the star due to its speed is measured through relativistic beaming. As the planet moves closer or further away from its host star, the brightness of the star varies and this gives clue for presence of planets.

Ellipsoidal variations-Massive planets orbiting their host stars can somewhat alter the star's shape. Because of this, the brightness of the star varies significantly depending on how it is rotated in relation to Earth.

Polarimetry-A polarised light reflected from the planet is distinguished from unpolarized light produced from the star using the polarimetry method. This approach has not identified any new planets, however it has spotted a few previously discovered planets.

Circumstellar disks-Many stars are surrounded by discs of cosmic dust thought to have formed from asteroids and comets colliding. Because the dust absorbs starlight and re-emits it as infrared radiation, it can be detected. The presence of planets may be indicated by features in the discs, however this is not regarded a conclusive detection method.

For the first time, the hue of an exoplanet was established in 2013. HD 189733b's best-fit measurements indicate that it is a deep dark blue. Later that year, the colours of numerous other exoplanets were identified, including GJ 504 b, which appears magenta in appearance, and Kappa Andromedae b, which appears reddish in appearance if seen up close. The appearance of helium planets is likely to be white or grey.

The way hydrogen evaporated from HD 209458 b suggested a magnetic field surrounding the planet in 2014. It's the first time an exoplanet's magnetic field has been detected (indirectly). The magnetic field is believed to be a tenth of the strength of Jupiter's.With sensitive enough radio telescopes like LOFAR, exoplanet magnetic fields could be detected by their auroral radio emissions.The radio emissions may allow for the measurement of an exoplanet's interior rotation rate, and may provide a more accurate method of measuring planetary rotation than observing cloud motion.

Exoplanets with atmospheres have been discovered. HD 209458 b was the first to be discovered in 2001.More than fifty transiting and five directly photographed exoplanet atmospheres have been seen as of February 2014, yielding molecular spectrum characteristics, day–night temperature gradients, and vertical atmospheric structure restrictions.

Exoplanetology is evolving into a more in-depth study of extrasolar worlds as additional planets are discovered, and will eventually address the possibility of life on planets beyond the Solar System.Exoplanets Kepler-62f, Kepler-186f, and Kepler-442b were recognised as the strongest candidates for being potentially habitable in a 2015 study. They are separated by 1200, 490, and 1,120 light-years, respectively. With a radius of 1.2 Earth-radius, Kepler-186f is similar in size to Earth, and it lies on the edge of the habitable zone orbiting its red dwarf star.

Life can only be discovered at cosmic distances if it has evolved on a planetary scale and has significantly altered the planetary environment. A potentially habitable planet must also orbit a stable star at a distance that allows planetary-mass objects with enough atmospheric pressure to support liquid water on their surfaces.

Minor planets

A minor planet is an astronomical object in direct orbit around the Sun or any other star with a planetary system that is neither a planet nor a comet.Near-Earth asteroids, Mars-crossers, main-belt asteroids, and Jupiter trojans are all minor planets, which are mostly found in the Kuiper belt and scattered disc.Since the 19th century, these objects have been referred to as minor planets. Planetoid is another term that has been used.

There are 1,086,655 known objects as of June 2021, classified into 567,132 numbered minor planets and 519,523 unnumbered minor planets.Ceres was the first minor planet identified in 1801. Within the Solar System, hundreds of thousands of small planets have been identified, with thousands more being discovered every month. The Minor Planet Center has recorded over 213 million sightings and 794,832 minor planets, 541,128 of which have orbits well enough known to be granted permanent official numbers.

Every astronomical body in the Solar System need its own designation. A three-step procedure is followed when naming minor planets. A provisionally labelled minor planet, for example, is given a temporary designation upon finding because the object could yet turn out to be a false positive or become lost later. A minor planet is formally identified and assigned a number once the observation arc is accurate enough to forecast its future location. It is then designated as a minor planet. Finally, it may be named by its discoverers in the third phase. Only a small percentage of minor planets have been given names. The great majority are either numbered or have a temporary designation.

Environmental characteristics are divided into three categories: space environment, surface environment, and internal environment, which include geological, optical, thermal, and radiological environmental properties, among others, and are used to understand the basic properties of minor planets, conduct scientific research, and design the payload of exploration missions.

The PDS Asteroid/Dust Archive contains data on the physical parameters of comets and small planets. This comprises binary system attributes, occultation timings and diameters, masses, densities, rotation periods, surface temperatures, albedoes, spin vectors, taxonomy, and absolute magnitudes and slopes, among other things. A Data Base on Physical and Dynamical Properties of Near Earth Asteroids is also maintained by the European Asteroid Research Node (E.A.R.N.), an alliance of asteroid research groups.

Some of these objects are thought to have only minor changes from their original state in the young solar nebula from which the planets formed, they could reveal information about planet Earth as well as the genesis and evolution of the solar system.Asteroids are small planets in our Solar System.

Asteroids

They are rocky or metallic bodies with no atmosphere. Asteroids, including dwarf planets, vary greatly in size and shape, but planets do not. Many asteroids are shattered fragments of planetesimals, things that never grew large enough to become planets within the early Sun's solar nebula. Planetesimals in the asteroid belt are assumed to have evolved similarly to the rest of the solar nebula's objects.

The bulk of known asteroids orbit between Mars and Jupiter in asteroid belts with low eccentricity (i.e. not extremely elongated) orbits. Between 1.1 and 1.9 million asteroids larger than 1 km (0.6 mi) in diameter, as well as millions of smaller ones, are thought to be contained inside this belt. These asteroids could be remnants of the protoplanetary disc, when Jupiter's massive gravitational perturbations prevented planetesimals from accreting into planets during the Solar System's formative phase.

Asteroids that pass close to Earth's orbit are known as near-Earth asteroids, or NEAs. Earth-crossers are asteroids that really cross Earth's orbital path. There are 28,772 near-Earth asteroids known as of April 2022.

Asteroids range in size from over 1000 km for the largest to 1 metre for the smallest. The three largest are nearly spherical, have partially separated interiors, and are assumed to be surviving protoplanets. The great majority, on the other hand, are much smaller and irregularly shaped, and are likely to be damaged planetesimals or fragments of larger things. The three largest objects, Ceres, Vesta, and Pallas, are entire protoplanets that share many properties common to planets and are atypical compared to the rest of irregularly shaped asteroids, despite their location in the asteroid belt.

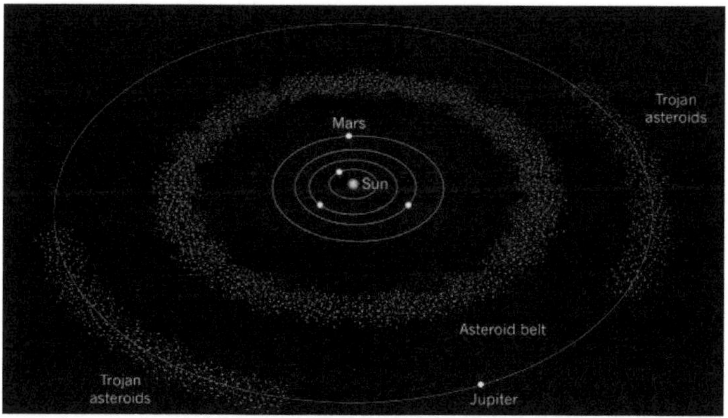

Asteroid belt

Objects in the asteroid belt could only be seen with enormous telescopes until the advent of space flight, and their shapes and topography remained a mystery. Only a modest amount of detail on the surfaces of the largest asteroids can be resolved by the best contemporary ground-based telescopes and the Earth-orbiting Hubble Space Telescope. Asteroids' light curves and spectral features can provide some information about their shapes and compositions, and asteroid sizes can be calculated by timing the lengths of star occultations. Particularly for near-Earth asteroids, radar imaging can provide useful information regarding asteroid morphologies, orbital and rotational properties. Flybys of spacecraft can provide far more data than ground- or space-based observations, and sample-return missions can reveal regolith composition.

Asteroids have been proposed as a supply of materials that are rare or exhausted on Earth,as well as materials for building space habitats. Asteroids may one day be mined for space manufacturing and construction materials that are too heavy and expensive to ship from Earth.

Asteroid prospecting could yield scientific data for the hunt for extraterrestrial intelligence from an astrobiological standpoint . Some astrophysicists believe that if intelligent extraterrestrial civilizations used asteroid mining in the past, the traces of their actions would still be visible now.

Asteroids contain residues of amino acids and other organic compounds, and some scientists believe that asteroid impacts may have seeded the early Earth with the molecules needed to start life, or perhaps brought life to Earth itself in a process known as "panspermia." DNA and RNA components may have been produced on asteroids and comets in outer space, according to a research published in August 2011 based on NASA studies with meteorites recovered on Earth.There is growing interest in locating asteroids whose orbits cross Earth's and potentially collide with the planet if given enough time. The Apollos, Amors, and Atens are the three most important groupings of near-Earth asteroids.

In terms of criteria like overall performance, cost, failure risks, operations, and technology readiness, different collision avoidance strategies have varying trade-offs. There are two types of strategies: fragmentation and delay. Fragmentation focuses on fragmenting the impactor and distributing the fragments such that they miss the Earth or are small enough to burn up in the atmosphere, rendering it harmless. Delay takes use of the fact that the Earth and the impactor are both in orbit. When both objects reach the same place in space at the same time, or more precisely, when some point on Earth's surface intersects the impactor's orbit when it arrives, an impact happens.

NASA, JAXA, ESA, and CNSA are all planning asteroid-dedicated missions.Lucy, NASA's first expedition to trojans, will launch in 2021 and will explore eight asteroids, one from the main belt, and seven Jupiter trojans. In 2027, the primary mission would begin. NASA's Double Asteroid Redirection Test (DART) was launched in November 2021 to test equipment for shielding Earth from potentially harmful objects. It will crash on the minor-planet moon Dimorphos of the twin asteroid Didymos in September 2022 to investigate the future potential of a spacecraft impact to deflect an asteroid on a collision course with Earth via momentum transfer. Hera, an ESA mission set to launch in 2024, will investigate the impact's findings.

Comets

The presence of an extensive, gravitationally unbound atmosphere surrounding the core nucleus distinguishes comets from asteroids. The coma -the centre component immediately around the nucleus and the tail -a generally linear section composed of dust or gas pushed out of the coma by the Sun's light pressure or outstreaming solar wind plasma are two distinct parts of this atmosphere.

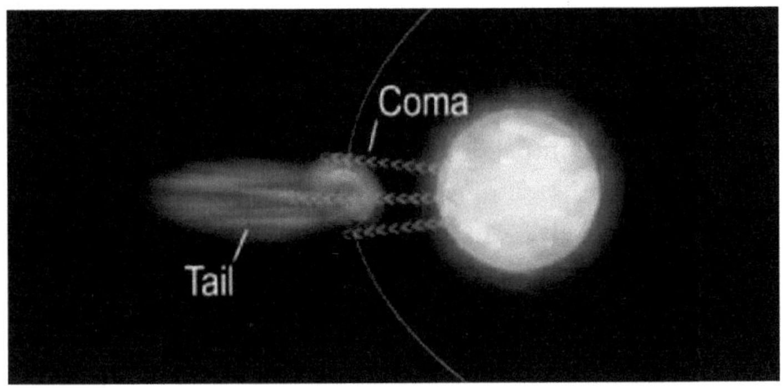

Comet near Sun

The majority of comets are small Solar System entities with elongated elliptical orbits that carry them near to the Sun for part of their orbit and then out into the Solar System's far reaches for the rest. The length of a comet's orbital period is typically used to classify it: the longer the period, the longer the ellipse.

Comets with orbital periods of less than 200 years are known as periodic comets or short-period comets. Long-period comets have orbits that are highly eccentric, with periods ranging from 200 years to thousands or possibly millions of years.

A comet gets bright enough to be spotted by a casual viewer about once every ten years, earning it the title of great comet. Predicting whether a comet will become a great comet is notoriously difficult, as several circumstances can cause the brightness of a comet to deviate significantly from expectations.

At perihelion, a sungrazing comet travels extremely close to the Sun, usually within a few million kilometres. Larger sungrazers can survive multiple perihelion crossings, whereas little sungrazers can be completely vaporised during such a near approach to the Sun. However, the high tidal forces they are subjected to frequently fragment them.

Exocomets have been discovered outside of the Solar System and may be common in the Milky Way. In 1987, an exocomet system was discovered orbiting Beta Pictoris, a young A-type main-sequence star. As of 2013, the absorption spectra created by enormous clouds of gas emitted by comets when they pass close to their star had discovered 11 such exocomet systems.

Many scientists believe that comets bombarding the infant Earth some 4 billion years ago brought the massive amounts of water that today fill the world's seas, or at least a large fraction of it. Others have questioned this theory.

The discovery of organic chemicals in substantial amounts in comets, particularly polycyclic aromatic hydrocarbons, has led to conjecture that comets or meteorites may have carried the precursors of life—or maybe life itself—to Earth. Impacts between rocky and icy surfaces, such as comets, were suggested in 2013 to have the capacity to generate the amino acids that make up proteins through shock synthesis.

There are 4584 known comets as of November 2021. However, because the reservoir of comet-like entities in the outer Solar System (the Oort cloud) is believed to be one trillion, this represents only a small proportion of the total possible comet population. Every year, about one comet is visible to the human eye, though many of them are feeble and uninteresting. "Great comets" are very luminous examples.

Unmanned probes have visited comets before, including Rosetta from the European Space Agency, which was the first to land a robotic spacecraft on a comet, and Deep Impact from NASA, which blew a crater on Comet Tempel 1 to explore its interior.The mission yielded results suggesting that the majority of a comet's water ice is below the surface and that these reservoirs feed the jets of vaporized water that form the coma of Tempel 1.

Materials obtained from the tail of Wild 2 were crystalline and could only have been "formed in fire" at temperatures exceeding 1,000 °C (1,830 °F), according to data from the Stardust mission. Although comets developed in the outer Solar System, it is hypothesised that radial mixing of material during the Solar System's early creation redistributed material throughout the proto-planetary disc.

Comets, as a result, include crystalline granules that originated in the early, heated Solar System. This can be found in both comet spectra and sample return missions. Even more recently, the recoverable elements show that "comet dust mimics asteroid materials." These new findings have caused scientists to reconsider the nature of comets and how they differ from asteroids.

Kuiper belt objects

The Kuiper belt is a circumstellar disc in the Solar System that extends from Neptune's orbit. It is mostly made up of tiny bodies or relics from the formation of the Solar System. While many asteroids are made mostly of rock and metal, the majority of Kuiper belt objects(KBOs) are made mostly of frozen volatiles like methane, ammonia, and water. Most of the objects that astronomers accept as dwarf planets are found in the Kuiper belt. The region may have given birth to some of the Solar System's moons, including Neptune's Triton and Saturn's Phoebe.

Kuiper belt

The Kuiper belt and Neptune can be used as indicators of the Solar System's size. Many theorised after Pluto's discovery in 1930 that it might not be alone. For decades, the Kuiper belt has been speculated about in various forms. The first direct evidence of its existence was discovered only in 1992. The Kuiper belt ranges from around 30–55 AU in its whole length (excluding the dispersed disc) and includes its outer areas.Because of orbital resonances, Neptune's presence has a significant impact on the Kuiper belt's structure. Neptune's gravity destabilises the orbits of any objects that chance to be in particular locations over a timescale comparable to the Solar System's age, and either sends them into the inner Solar System or out into the dispersed disc or interstellar space. As a result, the Kuiper belt's current layout has significant gaps.

The Kuiper belt's precise origins and complicated structure are unknown, and astronomers are waiting for the completion of numerous wide-field survey observatories, such as Pan-STARRS and the forthcoming LSST, which should uncover many previously unknown KBOs.Planetesimals, pieces of the original protoplanetary disc around the Sun that failed to fully consolidate into planets and instead created smaller things, the largest of which is less than 3,000 kilometres in diameter, are assumed to make up the Kuiper belt.

The traditional Kuiper belt appears to be made up of two distinct populations. The first, known as the "dynamically cold" population, has orbits that are almost circular and eccentric, similar to planets. The "dynamically hot" population, on the other hand, has orbits that are substantially more inclined to the ecliptic. The two populations were called after particles in a gas that increase their relative velocity as they become heated up, not because of any significant temperature differential.

The dynamically cold population is around 30 times less than the hot population. The hot population is thought to have developed near Neptune's original orbit and then dispersed during the large planets' migration.The cold population, on the other hand, is thought to have formed at roughly its current position due to the loose binaries' inability to survive contacts with Neptune.Many aspects of the Kuiper belt, such as "cold" and "hot" populations, resonant objects, and a scattered disc, are reproduced in the original form of the currently popular model, the "Nice model," but it still fails to account for some of the peculiarities of their distributions.

Kuiper belt objects, according to analysis, are made up of a mix of rock and a variety of ices, including water, methane, and ammonia. Since 2000, a number of KBOs have been discovered with diameters of 500 to 1,500 km (932 mi), more than half the size of Pluto (2370 km). 50000 Quaoar is a 1,200-kilometer-wide classical KBO discovered in 2002. Both Makemake and Haumea, both unveiled on July 29, 2005, are even bigger. Other objects, such as 28978 Ixion (found in 2001) and 20000 Varuna (discovered in 2000), are 600–700 kilometres (373–435 miles) in diameter.By 2006, astronomers have resolved dust discs around nine stars other than the Sun that were suspected to be Kuiper belt-like objects.

The finding of these big KBOs in orbits similar to Pluto's led many to believe that, aside from its size, Pluto was not that different from other Kuiper belt members. These objects are not just similar in size to Pluto, but many also have satellites and are composed similarly (methane and carbon monoxide have been found both on Pluto and on the largest KBOs). As a result, some speculated that Pluto, like Ceres, would be reclassified as a planet after the finding of its sibling asteroids.

Modern computer simulations demonstrate that Jupiter and Neptune had a substantial influence on the Kuiper belt, and that neither Uranus nor Neptune could have formed in their current positions since there was insufficient primordial matter in that range to build objects of such mass. These planets, on the other hand, are thought to have formed closer to Jupiter. Early in the Solar System's history, planetesimals scattered, causing the orbits of the major planets to migrate: Saturn, Uranus, and Neptune moved outwards, while Jupiter slid inwards.Kuiper belt objects are thought to be relatively unaffected by the processes that have shaped and altered other Solar System objects due to their distance from the Sun and major planets; thus, determining their composition would provide significant information on the makeup of the earliest Solar System.

ASTROBIOLOGY

CHAPTER FOUR

ASTROBIOLOGY

Astrobiology

Astrobiology or exobiology is an interdisciplinary field that studies the deterministic and contingent events that lead to the emergence, distribution, and evolution of life in the universe. It looks into whether or not extraterrestrial life exists, and if so, how humans can detect it.

Astrobiology combines molecular biology, biophysics, biochemistry, chemistry, astronomy, physical cosmology, exoplanetology, geology, palaeontology, and ichnology to examine the possibility of life on other worlds and aid in the identification of biospheres that may differ from Earth's.

Research on the origins of planetary systems, the origins of organic compounds in space, rock-water-carbon interactions, abiogenesis on Earth, planetary habitability, research on biosignatures for life detection, and studies on the potential for life to adapt to challenges on Earth and in space are all part of this interdisciplinary field.

Biochemistry may have originated shortly after the Big Bang, 13.8 billion years ago, during a period when the Universe was only 10–17 million years old, and during a habitable epoch when the Universe was only 10–17 million years old. According to the panspermia hypothesis, microscopic life may exist across the universe, dispersed by meteoroids, asteroids, and other small Solar System bodies.

Very big galaxies, according to research published in August 2015, may be more conducive to the formation and development of habitable planets than smaller galaxies like the Milky Way. Regardless, Earth is the only place in the cosmos where humans have discovered life. Estimates of habitable zones around other stars, dubbed "Goldilocks zones" by some, together with the finding of thousands of extrasolar planets and new insights into harsh habitats on Earth, suggest that there may be many more livable places in the cosmos than previously thought conceivable.

Even if extraterrestrial life is never discovered, astrobiology's interdisciplinary character, as well as the cosmic and evolutionary perspectives it fosters, may result in a variety of benefits here on Earth.

Gavriil Tikhov, a Russian (Soviet) astronomer, coined the phrase in 1953. Exobiology is thought to have a narrow scope limited to the search for life outside of Earth, whereas astrobiology is a broader field that studies the relationship between life and the universe, which includes the search for extraterrestrial life as well as the study of life on Earth, its origin, evolution, and limits.

The topic of whether life exists elsewhere in the cosmos is a provable hypothesis and hence a valid area of scientific study, despite the fact that it is a new and developing field. Astrobiology has become a codified branch of study, despite being originally deemed outside the mainstream of scientific investigation. Astrobiology, according to planetary scientist David Grinspoon, is a branch of natural philosophy that grounds speculation on the unknown in established scientific theory.

NASA's interest in exobiology dates back to the early days of the United States Space Program. NASA financed its first exobiology project in 1959, and in 1960, it established an Exobiology Program, which is now one of NASA's four core components of the present Astrobiology Program. NASA funded the search for extraterrestrial intelligence (SETI) in 1971 to look for interstellar communications broadcast by extraterrestrial life outside the Solar System using radio frequencies in the electromagnetic spectrum. Three biology experiments were included in NASA's Viking missions to Mars, which launched in 1976 and were supposed to look for current life on Mars.

The majority of astronomy-related astrobiology research focuses on finding extrasolar planets (exoplanets), with the assumption that if life evolved on Earth, it may also exist on other planets with similar properties. A variety of detectors designed to identify Earth-sized exoplanets have been considered for this purpose, the most notable of which are NASA's Terrestrial Planet Finder (TPF) and ESA's Darwin missions, both of which have been cancelled.

In March 2009, NASA began the Kepler space project, and in 2006, the French Satellite Agency launched the COROT space mission. Several less ambitious ground-based projects are also underway. These missions are designed to not only find Earth-sized planets, but also to detect light from them so that they may be investigated spectroscopically. It would be able to establish the basic composition of an extrasolar planet's atmosphere and/or surface by analysing planetary spectra. With this information, it may be feasible to estimate the chances of finding life on that planet.

The Synthetic Planet Laboratory, a NASA research group, is utilising computer modelling to create a range of virtual worlds to explore how they would appear to TPF or Darwin. Once these missions are operational, it is intended that their spectra may be compared to these synthetic planetary spectra to look for traits that might suggest the presence of life.

Life was assumed to be fully reliant on solar energy until the 1970s. Plants on the Earth's surface use sunlight to photosynthesize carbohydrates from carbon dioxide and water, producing oxygen that is then eaten by oxygen-respiring creatures, transmitting energy up the food chain. Even life in the ocean depths, where sunlight cannot reach, was assumed to eat organic debris rained down from the surface waters or eat animals that did. The ability of the world to maintain life was assumed to be dependent on its ability to receive sunlight.

Scientists spotted colonies of enormous tube worms, clams, crabs, mussels, and other miscellaneous organisms concentrated around undersea volcanic structures known as black smokers during an exploratory trip to the Galapagos Rift in the deep-sea exploration submersible Alvin in 1977. Despite the lack of sunshine, these animals thrive, and it was soon revealed that they form a self-contained ecosystem. Although most of these multicellular lifeforms require dissolved oxygen produced by oxygenic photosynthesis for aerobic cellular respiration and thus are not completely self-sufficient in terms of sunlight, the foundation of their food chain is a type of bacterium that gets its energy from the oxidation of reactive chemicals such as hydrogen or hydrogen sulphide that bubble up from the Earth's interior.

Green sulphur bacteria that capture geothermal light for anoxygenic photosynthesis or bacteria that perform chemolithoautotrophy based on the radioactive decay of uranium are examples of lifeforms that are completely divorced from the energy from sunlight. This chemosynthesis revolutionized biology and astrobiology by proving that life does not need the sun to exist; all it needs is water and an energy gradient.

Extremophiles have been discovered in ice, boiling water, acid, alkali, nuclear reactor water cores, salt crystals, hazardous waste, and a variety of other extreme habitats previously thought to be unfriendly to life. This ushered in a new era of astrobiology by vastly increasing the number of potential alien habitats. Grasp how life might emerge elsewhere in the cosmos requires a thorough understanding of these species, their surroundings, and their evolutionary paths. The lichen fungi Rhizocarpon geographicum and Xanthoria elegans, the bacteria Bacillus safensis, Deinococcus radiodurans, Bacillus subtilis, yeast Saccharomyces cerevisiae, Arabidopsis thaliana ('mouse-ear cress') seeds, and the invertebrate animal Tardigrade are just a few examples of organisms that can withstand the vacuum and radiation of outer space.

While tardigrades are not true extremophiles, they are extremotolerant microorganisms that have made significant contributions to the science of astrobiology. Their high radiation resistance and existence of DNA protection proteins may hold the key to determining if life can live outside of the Earth's protective atmosphere.Due to their deep water oceans where radiogenic and tidal heating allows liquid water to exist, Jupiter's moon Europa and Saturn's moon Enceladus are presently regarded the most plausible locations for existent extraterrestrial life.

Abiogenesis, or the origin of life, is a subject of study that is different from the evolution of life. The conditions on the early Earth, according to Oparin and Haldane, were favourable for the creation of organic molecules from inorganic elements, and hence for the formation of many of the chemicals found in all forms of life today. Although research into this process, known as prebiotic chemistry, has progressed, it remains uncertain whether life could have started in this manner on Earth.

The alternate concept of panspermia is that the earliest elements of life may have developed on another planet with even better conditions, or perhaps in interstellar space, asteroids, and other bodies, and then been transported to Earth.

Panspermia hypothesis

Complex organic compounds ("amorphous organic solids with a mixed aromatic-aliphatic structure") that could be generated naturally and swiftly by stars are found in cosmic dust. Furthermore, a scientist speculated that these compounds could have played a role in the evolution of life on Earth, stating, "If this is the case, life on Earth may have had an easier time getting started as these organics can serve as basic components for life."

Polycyclic aromatic hydrocarbons (PAHs), which could be the starting elements for the development of life, could account for more than 20% of the carbon in the universe. PAHs appear to have created soon after the Big Bang, are found everywhere in the cosmos, and are linked to nascent stars and exoplanets. PAHs are exposed to interstellar medium conditions and changed into more complex organics via hydrogenation, oxygenation, and hydroxylation—a step toward amino acids and nucleotides, the basic ingredients of proteins and DNA, respectively.

Astroecology

The interactions of life with space habitats and resources on planets, asteroids, and comets are studied in astroecology. Astroecology, on a broader scale, is concerned with the availability of resources for life around stars in the galaxy in the cosmic future. Astroecology is a branch of astrobiology that aims to measure future life in space.

Using actual space elements found in meteorites, experimental astroecology studies resources in planetary soils. The findings imply that bacteria, algae, and plant (asparagus, potato) cultures can thrive in Martian and carbonaceous chondrite materials with high soil fertility. The findings suggest that life could have persisted in early wet asteroids and comparable materials brought to Earth by dust, comets, and meteorites, and that these asteroid materials could be used as soil for future space colonies.

Cosmoecology is the study of life in the cosmos over cosmic timescales. Red giant stars and white and red dwarf stars may be the primary sources of energy, supporting life for billions of years. Astroecologists believe that their mathematical models will be able to calculate the potential amounts of future life in space, allowing for a comparable rise in biodiversity, which might lead to a broad range of intelligent life forms.

Astrogeology

Astrogeology is a branch of planetary science that studies the geology of celestial bodies such planets, moons, asteroids, comets, and meteorites. This discipline's data enables for the assessment of a planet's or natural satellite's ability to develop and sustain life, or planetary habitability.

Geochemistry is a branch of astrogeology that studies the chemical composition of the Earth and other planets, as well as the chemical processes and reactions that govern the composition of rocks and soils, as well as the cycles of matter and energy and their interactions with the planet's hydrosphere and atmosphere. Cosmochemistry, biochemistry, and organic geochemistry are some of the specialisations available.

The oldest known evidence for life on Earth is found in the fossil record. Paleontologists can better comprehend the types of animals that arose on the early Earth by studying fossil evidence. Some locations on Earth, such as Western Australia's Pilbara and Antarctica's McMurdo Dry Valleys, are thought to be geological analogues to regions on Mars, and hence could provide hints on how to search for previous life on Mars.

The numerous organic functional groups, which are made up of hydrogen, oxygen, nitrogen, phosphorus, sulphur, and a variety of metals including iron, magnesium, and zinc, enable a living cell to catalyse a tremendous variety of chemical processes. In contrast to the combinatorial cosmos of organic macromolecules, silicon interacts with only a few other atoms, thus big silicon molecules are monotonous.

In principle, it appears plausible that the basic building elements of life will be comparable to those on Earth. Although terrestrial life and life that may originate independently of Earth are likely to share many comparable, if not identical, building components, they are also expected to have some biological characteristics that are distinct. If life has had a similar impact elsewhere in the Solar System, the relative abundances of substances critical to its survival—whatever they may be—could be a sign of its presence. Whatever extraterrestrial life may be, its proclivity for chemically altering its surroundings may be a dead giveaway.

Astrobotany

Astrobotany is the study of plants in space habitats, which is an applied sub-discipline of botany. It is a branch of botany and astrobiology.Plants can be grown in space, often in a weightless but pressurised controlled atmosphere in specific space gardens, according to research. They can be used as food and/or produce a pleasant atmosphere in the context of human spaceflight. Plants can assist control cabin humidity by metabolising carbon dioxide in the air to provide essential oxygen. Human spaceflight personnel may benefit psychologically from growing plants in space.

The first issue in growing plants in space is figuring out how to get them to grow in the absence of gravity. This presents complications in terms of the impact of gravity on root development, as well as the provision of suitable lighting and other issues.

The nutrient delivery to roots, nutrient biogeochemical cycles, and microbiological interactions in soil-based substrates are particularly complex, but they have been shown to make space farming in hypo- and microgravity conceivable.NASA intends to cultivate plants in space to help feed astronauts while also providing psychological benefits for long-term space travel.Gavriil Tikhov was the first to try to discover extraterrestrial flora by studying the wavelengths of a planet's reflected light, or planetshine. Photosynthetic pigments, like chlorophylls on Earth, have light spectra that peak between 700 and 750 nanometers.

The "vegetation's red edge" is the name given to this prominent spike. It was anticipated that a surge in planetshine readings would indicate a surface covered in green vegetation. The quest for microbial life on other planets or mathematical models to forecast the possibility of life on exoplanets has trumped the search for alien greenery.Astrobotany research also includes the study of plant reaction in space conditions. Plants in space face unique environmental stressors that they don't face on Earth, such as microgravity, ionising radiation, and oxidative stress. Experiments have indicated that these stresses change plant metabolism pathways genetically. Plants respond to their environment on a molecular level, as evidenced by changes in genetic expression. Astrobotanical research has been used to address the issues of developing life support systems in space and on other worlds, most notably Mars.

Hypothetical food production in Mars

One of the first people to consider exploiting photosynthetic life as a resource in space agriculture systems was Russian scientist Konstantin Tsiolkovsky. Plant cultivation in space has been discussed since the early twentieth century. Gavriil Adrianovich Tikhov, a Soviet astronomer and astrobiology pioneer, coined the term astrobotany in 1945. Tikhov is regarded as the founder of astrobiology. Growing Earth plants in space conditions and seeking for botanical life on other planets have both been studied in this topic.

The first creatures in space were "specially cultivated strains of seeds" carried to a distance of 134 kilometres (83 miles) on July 9, 1946, by a V-2 rocket launched from the United States. There was no way to get these samples back. Maize seeds were the first to be launched into space and safely recovered on July 30, 1946, and were quickly followed by rye and cotton.

The Naval Research Laboratory and Harvard University were in charge of these early suborbital biological investigations, which were concerned with radiation damage on live tissue. On Apollo 14, 500 tree seeds were flown around the Moon in 1971 (Loblolly pine, Sycamore, Sweetgum, Redwood, and Douglas fir). These Moon trees were planted and cultivated in a controlled environment on Earth, with no noticeable modifications.

On the International Space Station, plant study continued. The Biomass Production System was utilised on Expedition 4 of the International Space Station. Later, the Vegetable Production System (Veggie) was utilised on the International Space Station (ISS). Before heading into space, lettuce, Swiss chard, radishes, Chinese cabbage, and peas were all tested in Veggie.

On Expedition 40, red Romaine lettuce was grown in space, picked when mature, frozen, and tested on Earth. When their crop of Red Romaine was harvested on August 10, 2015, Expedition 44 members became the first American astronauts to eat plants cultivated in space. Russian cosmonauts have been consuming half of their crop since 2003, while the other half is used for study. A sunflower grew aboard the International Space Station in 2012, thanks to NASA astronaut Donald Pettit's care. One of the goals is to grow food for crew consumption.

Radish in International Space Station

Algae was the initial candidate for life support systems for humans and plants. Chlorella, Anacystis, Synechocystis, Scenedesmus, Synechococcus, and Spirulina species were employed in early studies in the 1950s and 1960s to investigate how photosynthetic organisms may be exploited for O2 and CO2 cycling in closed systems.Starch crops like wheat, potato, and rice; protein-rich crops like soy, peanut, and common bean; and a slew of other nutrient-dense crops like lettuce, strawberry, and kale are among the most commonly studied.Tests for the best growing circumstances in closed systems necessitated study into both environmental factors required for certain crops (such as different light times for short-day versus long-day crops) and cultivars best-suited to life support system growth.

Recent studies have focused on projecting these life support systems to other planets, including Martian colonies. On the Martian surface, interlocking closed systems known as "modular biospheres" have been prototyped to accommodate four to five-person crews. These encampments are designed to serve as greenhouses and bases for inflatable greenhouses.

They'll likely employ Martian soils for growth substrate and wastewater treatment, as well as crop varieties designed expressly for extraterrestrial life. There has also been talk of using the Martian moon Phobos as a resource base, with the possibility of extracting frozen water and carbon dioxide from the surface, as well as exploiting hollowed craters for autonomous growth chambers that may be gathered during mining expeditions.Plant research has provided information that has been valuable in various areas of botany and horticulture. NASA conducted extensive study into hydroponics systems, as well as the impacts of increasing photoperiod and light intensity for diverse crop species, as part of the CELSS and ALS programmes. In addition, research led to yield optimizations that were previously unattainable by indoor cropping systems.

Intensive research into gas exchange and plant volatile concentrations in closed systems has resulted in a better knowledge of how plants react to high quantities of gases like carbon dioxide and ethylene. The expanding usage of LEDs in indoor growing operations has been motivated by research into the use of LEDs in closed life support systems.Experiments take a broader approach to examining plant growth patterns rather than focusing on a single growth trait.For example, the Canadian Space Agency discovered that white spruce seedlings grew differently in the anti-gravity space environment than they did on Earth; the space seedlings had enhanced growth from the shoots and needles and randomised amyloplast distribution, when compared to the Earth-bound control group.

Assumptions

Some simplifying assumptions can help astrobiologists lessen the magnitude of their assignment while seeking for life on other worlds like Earth. One is the well-informed notion that the vast majority of life forms in our galaxy, as well as all life forms on Earth, are based on carbon chemistry. Carbon is famous for the extremely large number of molecules that can be created around it.

Carbon is the fourth most plentiful element in the universe, and the amount of energy necessary to form or break a bond is just right for creating molecules that are both stable and reactive. Carbon atoms may easily connect to other carbon atoms, allowing for the construction of incredibly lengthy and complex compounds.

Liquid water is a given because it is a common molecule that provides an ideal environment for the development of complex carbon-based compounds that could potentially lead to the advent of life. Some researchers propose water-ammonia combination settings as suitable solvents for hypothetical biochemistry.

A third assumption is that planets circling Sun-like stars have a higher probability of becoming habitable. Life may not have enough time to emerge on planets orbiting very massive stars due to their short lives. Only planets in very close orbits around very small stars would not be frozen solid, and these planets would be tidally "locked" to the star since they supply so little heat and warmth. Because red dwarfs have such lengthy lives, they may be able to generate livable habitats on planets with thick atmospheres. Red dwarfs are extremely prevalent, thus this is noteworthy.

The Viking programme and the Beagle 2 missions were expressly designed to look for present life on Mars. The

Viking results were equivocal, and minutes after landing, Beagle 2 failed. The Jupiter Icy Moons Orbiter, which was supposed to research Jupiter's icy moons—some of which may have liquid water—would have been a future mission with a major astrobiology function if it hadn't been cancelled. The Phoenix lander, launched in late 2008, investigated the climate on Mars for past and present planetary habitability of microbial life, as well as the history of water.

The European Space Agency's astrobiology strategy, published in 2016, listed five major study areas and many key scientific objectives for each.

1) Origin and evolution of planetary systems

2) Origins of organic compounds in space

3) Rock-water-carbon interactions, organic synthesis on Earth, and stages to life

4) Life and habitability

5) Biosignatures as a means of detecting life.

NASA launched the Mars Science Laboratory mission in November 2011, carrying the Curiosity rover, which landed on Mars in August 2012 at Gale Crater. On December 9, 2013, NASA announced that Gale Crater included an old freshwater lake that could have been a suitable environment for microbial life, based on findings from Curiosity's analysis of Aeolis Palus.The European Space Agency is currently working on the ExoMars astrobiology rover with the Russian Federal Space Agency (Roscosmos), which was supposed to launch in July 2020 but was pushed back to 2022. In the meantime, NASA launched the Mars 2020 astrobiology rover and sample cacher, which will return to Earth at a later date.

ASTROCHEMISTRY

CHAPTER FIVE

ASTROCHEMISTRY

Astrochemistry

The study of the abundance and reactivity of molecules in the Universe, as well as their interactions with radiation, is known as astrochemistry. The field is a combination of astronomy and chemistry. Both the Solar System and the interstellar medium are covered under the term "astrochemistry." Cosmochemistry is the study of the abundance of elements and isotope ratios in Solar System objects such as meteorites, while molecular astrophysics is the study of interstellar atoms and molecules and their interactions with radiation. The origin, atomic and chemical composition, history, and fate of molecular gas clouds are of particular interest since solar systems are formed from these clouds.

The history of astrochemistry is based on the shared history of the two disciplines as an extension of astronomy and chemistry. The advancement of both observational and experimental spectroscopy has enabled the discovery of a growing number of molecules within solar systems and the interstellar medium. As a result of advances in spectroscopy and other technologies, the number of chemicals found has expanded, expanding the chemical space available for astrochemical research.

While radio astronomy was developed in the 1930s, no considerable evidence for the definite identification of an interstellar molecule came until 1937. Up until this time, the only chemical species known to exist in interstellar space were atomic. McKellar et al. found and attributed spectroscopic lines in an as-yet unnamed radio observation to CH and CN molecules in interstellar space in 1940, confirming their findings. A small number of other molecules were discovered in interstellar space over the next thirty years, the most notable of which were OH, discovered in 1963 and important as a source of interstellar oxygen,and H2CO (Formaldehyde), discovered in 1969 and significant for being the first observed organic, polyatomic molecule in interstellar space.

Some regard the finding of interstellar formaldehyde – and later other molecules with potential biological relevance like water or carbon monoxide – as strong evidence for abiogenetic theories of life, which maintain that life's core molecular components come from extraterrestrial origins. This has prompted a continuing search for interstellar molecules that are either directly biologically important – such as interstellar glycine, discovered in 2009 – or that exhibit biologically relevant properties such as Chirality – one example of which (propylene oxide) was discovered in 2016 alongside more basic astrochemical research.

Spectroscopy, which uses telescopes to measure the absorption and emission of light from molecules and atoms in diverse settings, is an important experimental method in astrochemistry. Astrochemists can estimate the elemental abundances, chemical composition, and temperatures of stars and interstellar clouds by combining astronomical observations with laboratory measurements.

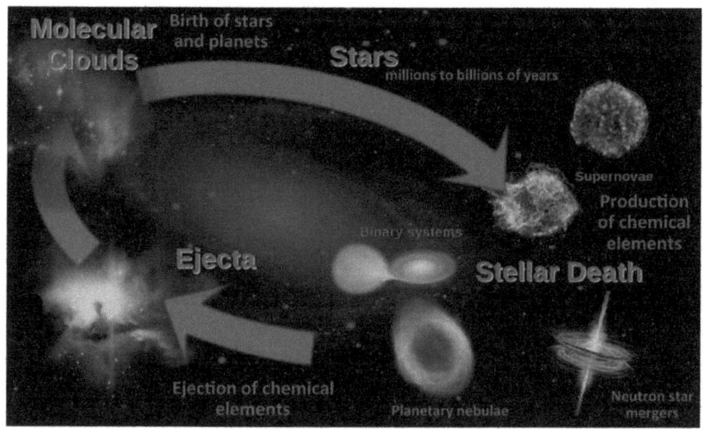

The cosmic cycle of chemical matter in a galaxy

This is conceivable because ions, atoms, and molecules have distinct spectra, or the absorption and emission of specific wavelengths (colours) of light, which are frequently invisible to the naked sight. However, depending on the chemical properties of the molecules, different forms of radiation (radio, infrared, visible, ultraviolet, etc.) can detect only particular types of species. The first organic molecule discovered in the interplanetary medium was interstellar formaldehyde.

Radio astronomy, which has resulted in the detection of over a hundred interstellar species, including radicals and ions, as well as organic i.e. carbon-based molecules such as alcohols, acids, aldehydes, and ketones, is perhaps the most potent tool for detecting particular chemical species. CO is one of the most numerous interstellar molecules, and due to its large electric dipole moment, one of the easiest to detect with radio waves (carbon monoxide). CO is so ubiquitous in interstellar space that it's even utilised to map out molecular areas.

The claim of interstellar glycine, the simplest amino acid, is possibly the radio observation of greatest human interest, yet it is accompanied by substantial debate. One of the reasons for the controversy surrounding this discovery is that, while radio and other approaches such as rotational spectroscopy are good at identifying simple species with large dipole moments, they are less sensitive to more complex molecules, even something as small as amino acids.

Polyaromatic hydrocarbons, also known as PAHs or PACs, are a class of complex gas-phase carbon molecules discovered by infrared astronomy in the interstellar medium. These molecules, which are predominantly made up of fused carbon rings in either a neutral or ionised form, are thought to be the most prevalent type of carbon compound in the universe. They're also the most frequent type of carbon molecule in meteorites and cosmic dust from comets and asteroids. These chemicals, as well as amino acids, nucleobases, and a variety of other compounds found in meteorites, contain deuterium and carbon, nitrogen, and oxygen isotopes that are extremely rare on Earth, indicating that they came from another planet. PAHs are thought to develop in the heated circumstellar environments that surround dying, carbon-rich red giant stars.

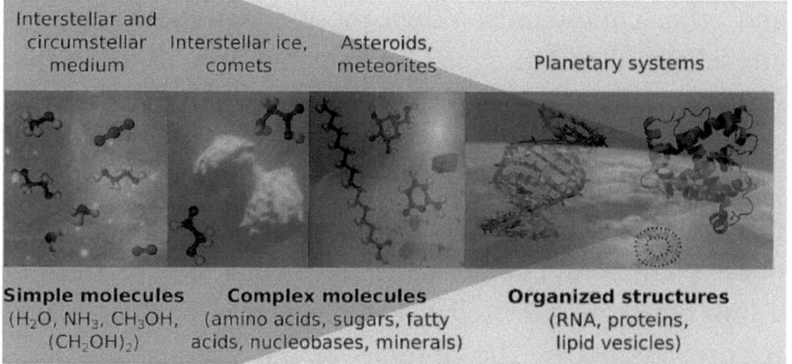

Simple and complex molecules in space

The composition of solid materials in the interstellar medium, such as silicates, kerogen-like carbon-rich solids, and ices, has also been determined via infrared astronomy. This is because, unlike visible light, which is scattered or absorbed by solid particles, infrared radiation can travel through minuscule interstellar particles, yet there are absorptions at specific wavelengths that are distinctive of the grains' composition. There are several restrictions, like with radio astronomy, for example, N2 is difficult to detect using either IR or radio astronomy.

Thin ice layers wrap the microscopic particles in dense clouds when there are enough particles to attenuate the harmful UV light, allowing some low-temperature chemistry to occur, according to IR observations. The chemistry of these ices is governed by the chemistry of hydrogen, which is by far the most abundant molecule in the universe. If the hydrogen is atomic, the H atoms react with the available O, C, and N atoms to form "reduced" species such as H2O, CH4, and NH3. If the hydrogen is molecular and hence not reactive, the heavier atoms can react or remain linked together, resulting in CO, CO2, CN, and other compounds. When these mixed-molecular ices are subjected to ultraviolet and cosmic rays, they develop intricate radiation-driven chemistry.

Amino acids have been synthesised in lab tests on the photochemistry of simple interstellar ices. The resemblance of interstellar and cometary ices, as well as gas phase compound comparisons, have been used as signs of a link between interstellar and cometary chemistry. This is corroborated by the findings of the Stardust mission's examination of organics from comet fragments, but the minerals also revealed a surprise contribution from high-temperature chemistry in the solar nebula.

In analysing the nuclear reactions that occur in stars, as well as the structure of stellar interiors, astrochemistry intersects with astrophysics and nuclear physics. Dredge-up events can occur if a star develops a predominantly convective envelope, bringing the products of nuclear burning to the surface. Expelled material may contain molecules whose rotational and vibrational spectrum changes can be seen with radio and infrared observatories if the star is losing a lot of mass.

The collection of carbon stars with silicate and water-ice outer envelopes is an interesting illustration of this. We can watch these stars evolving from an original composition in which oxygen was more plentiful than carbon to a carbon star phase in which the carbon produced by helium burning is transported to the surface by deep convection, significantly changing the molecular makeup of the stellar wind.

Scientists stated in October 2011 that cosmic dust contains organic stuff -amorphous organic solids with a mixed aromatic-aliphatic structure that might be produced organically and quickly by stars.Astronomers from Copenhagen University revealed the discovery of an unique sugar molecule, glycolaldehyde, in a distant star system on August 29, 2012, in a world first. The molecule was discovered 400 light years from Earth, near the protostellar pair IRAS 16293-2422. Glycolaldehyde is required for the formation of ribonucleic acid, or RNA, which functions similarly to DNA. This discovery shows that complex organic molecules may originate in star systems before planets form, eventually arriving on young planets early in their formation.

NASA announced in February 2014 the construction of a new spectral database for tracking polycyclic aromatic hydrocarbons (PAHs) throughout the universe. According to scientists, PAHs may account for more than 20% of the carbon in the cosmos, making them potential starting ingredients for the genesis of life. PAHs appear to have created soon after the Big Bang, are found everywhere around the cosmos, and are linked to new stars and exoplanets.

In July 2015, scientists stated that measurements by the COSAC and Ptolemy sensors revealed sixteen chemical molecules on comet 67/P's surface, four of which were seen for the first time on a comet, including acetamide, acetone, methyl isocyanate, and propionaldehyde.The Astrophysics and Astrochemistry Laboratory's experts have participated in space missions and conducted astronomical observations with telescopes such as the Hubble and Spitzer Space Telescopes, the Kuiper Airborne Observatory (KAO), and the NASA IRTF and NOAO Kitt Peak Telescopes.

Astrochemistry is also used in the study of star and planet atmospheres. Current and future observatories will hunt for molecules like water and carbon compounds to discover the chemical constituents that make up planetary atmospheres.Astrochemistry is crucial because it enables us to comprehend the abundance and evolution of chemical elements and molecules in the universe.

Understanding the chemistry that occurs in space, i.e., how molecules form and evolve, could assist to set the stage for understanding the emergence of life on Earth and beyond. This element of Astrochemistry has attracted the curiosity of the entire scientific community, but knowledge is still in its infancy.

ASTROMETRY

CHAPTER SIX

ASTROMETRY

Astrometry is the study of the precise locations and motions of stars and other celestial bodies. Near-Earth objects are tracked using astrometric techniques by astronomers. Many record-breaking Solar System objects have been discovered, thanks to astrometry. Astronomers use telescopes to survey the sky and large-area cameras to capture photos at various intervals to find such things astrometrically. They can discover Solar System objects by observing their movements in relation to the fixed background stars in these photographs.It explains the kinematics and physical origins of the Solar System and the Milky Way galaxy.

Astrometry's history is intertwined with that of star catalogues, which provided astronomers with reference locations for celestial objects so they could trace their movements. This can be traced back to Hipparchus, who discovered Earth's precession in 190 BC using the records of his predecessors Timocharis and Aristillus.

Tycho Brahe employed better devices, particularly enormous mural instruments, in the 16th century to estimate star positions more precisely than before. The European Space Agency's Hipparcos satellite launched astrometry into orbit in 1989, where it was less impacted by

Earth's mechanical forces and visual distortions. Hipparcos was an optical telescope that operated from 1989 to 1993 and measured big and tiny angles on the sky with far more precision than any previous optical telescope. 118,218 stars' locations, parallaxes, and proper motions were measured with remarkable precision over its 4-year operation.

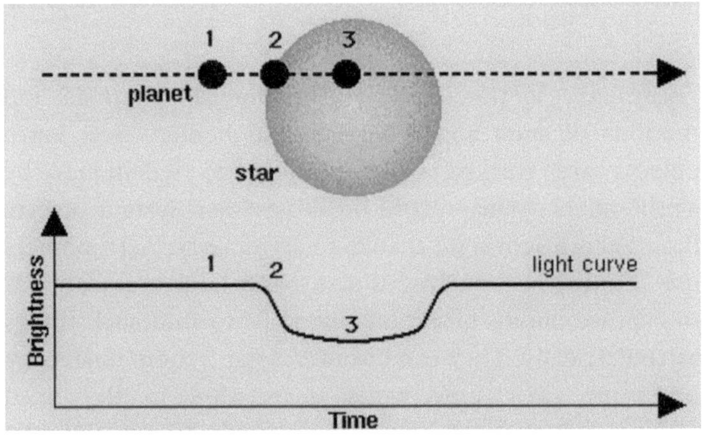

Drop in brightness when a planet pass in front of their parent star

Astrometry is essential for subjects such as celestial mechanics, star dynamics, and galactic astronomy, in addition to providing astronomers with a reference frame in which to describe their findings. Astrometric techniques are used in observational astronomy to assist identify star objects by their distinctive movements.Astrometry has also been used to back up claims of extrasolar planet discovery by measuring the shift in their parent star's apparent position on the sky caused by their shared orbit around the system's centre of mass. Astrometry is more precise in space missions that are not impacted by the Earth's atmosphere's distortions.

Astrometry is a technique for precisely measuring a star's position in the sky and tracking how it changes over time. Initially, this is accomplished by seeing and measuring the periodic wobble that a planet causes in the location of its parent star. The two-body problem is the wobbling of a planet in a stellar system. When a planet is in the gravitational system pull of another planet or star system, the greater gravitational pull dominates, but the lesser gravitational pull has an influence on the object with the stronger gravitational attraction.The wobbling is the process of a star and planet revolving around their common centre of mass (barycenter). Because the star is much more massive, its orbit will be much smaller, and the shared centre of mass will, in most situations, be within the radius of the larger body.

Only very massive exoplanets can be found using the wobbling method. The wobble generated by Earth-like objects is too slight to be recorded by present detectors, hence Earth-like planets could not be identified this way.

The astrometric technique has the benefit of being most sensitive to planets with big orbits. As a result, it can be used in conjunction with other approaches that are more sensitive to planets with small orbits. However, because planets far enough from their star to be detected using astrometry need a long time to complete an orbit, very extended observation times will be necessary – years, if not decades.

Astrophysicists employ astrometric observations to limit certain celestial mechanics theories. It is feasible to set a limit on the asymmetry of supernova explosions by measuring the velocities of pulsars. Astrometric data are also used to figure out where dark matter is distributed in the galaxy.

Gaia, a space-based observatory launched in 2013, is projected to find thousands of planets by astrometry, however no planet detected by astrometry had been confirmed prior to Gaia's launch.

Error correction is an important part of astrometry. Various factors, like as atmospheric conditions, instrument defects, and errors by the observer or measuring devices, induce inaccuracies into the measurement of star locations. Many of these errors can be eliminated using a variety of strategies, including instrument modifications and data compensations. Following that, statistical methods are used to compute data estimates and error ranges.

Photometry

Photometry is an astronomical technique that involves measuring the flux or intensity of light emitted by celestial objects.Differential photometry, which measures the brightness of a target item and nearby stars in the starfield at the same time, and relative photometry, which compares the brightness of a target object to stars with known fixed magnitudes, are both utilised in the observation of variable stars. Surface photometry can also be used to measure the apparent magnitude of extended objects like planets, comets, nebulae, and galaxies.

To do differential photometry, one must account for variations in the instrument's sensitivity over time as well as changes in the extinction of the atmosphere through which the object is examined (when observing from the ground). This is often accomplished by simultaneously observing a number of constant comparison stars with the object(s) of interest.

To do relative photometry, one must account for spatial changes in the instrument's sensitivity as well as air extinction. This is sometimes done in addition to adjusting for temporal differences, especially when the objects being compared are too far apart on the sky to be observed simultaneously.

To accomplish absolute photometry, variations between the effective passband through which an item is observed and the passband used to construct the standard photometric system must be corrected.

In the ultraviolet, visible, and infrared wavelengths of the electromagnetic spectrum, photometers use specialised standard passband filters. A photometric system is any set of filters with established light transmission properties that can be used to determine certain properties about stars and other celestial objects.

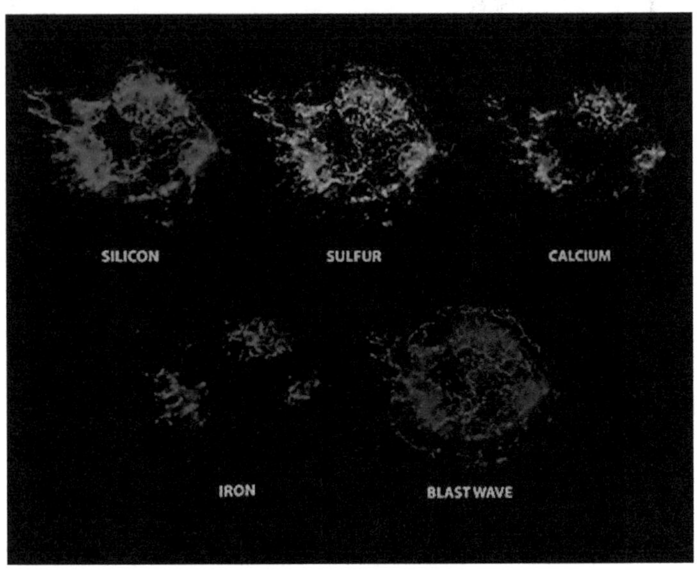

A variety of filters allows for focusing on one specific wavelength range at a time

When light from a star is collected by a telescope, it is focused onto a small microchip inside a charged-coupled device (CCD). This microprocessor is made up of a huge grid of light-sensing pixels .

When light strikes a pixel, the atoms within it release electrons, causing the pixel to become charged. This is known as photoionization.The pixel's number of liberated electrons is proportional to the number of incoming photons.

The number of electrons in each pixel is counted and read by a computer as counts or intensity at the end of the exposure. This processis utilised to calculate the apparent magnitude of the object.The brighter the star, the more electrons are released from the pixels and therefore the higher the counts or intensity.

Photometric systems are employed in a variety of astronomical applications. If an object's distance can be determined, photometric observations can be coupled with the inverse-square law to infer its luminosity, or its distance if its luminosity is known.

Photometry is also used to investigate the light variations of objects like variable stars, minor planets, active galactic nuclei, and supernovae, as well as to find transiting extrasolar planets.

The orbital period and radii of members of an eclipsing binary star system, the rotation period of a small planet or a star, and the overall energy output of supernovae may all be determined using measurements of these fluctuations.

Spectroscopy

In the electromagnetic spectrum, astronomical spectroscopy is used to measure three major bands of radiation: visible light, radio waves, and X-rays.

Many other sorts of celestial objects, including as planets, nebulae, galaxies, and active galactic nuclei, are studied using spectroscopy.

There are two types of spectrometry .

- Optical spectroscopy
- Radio spectroscopy

While all spectroscopy looks at certain parts of the spectrum, depending on the frequency, different methods are required to acquire the signal.A stellar spectrum can disclose information on a star's chemical composition, temperature, density, mass, distance, and luminosity, among other things. By measuring the Doppler shift, spectroscopy can reveal the velocity of motion towards or away from the observer.

While all spectroscopy looks at certain parts of the spectrum, depending on the frequency, different methods are required to acquire the signal. Ozone (O3) and molecular oxygen (O2) absorb light with wavelengths less than 300 nm, necessitating the employment of a satellite telescope or rocket-mounted detectors for X-ray and ultraviolet spectroscopy. The wavelengths of radio signals are substantially longer than those of optical signals, necessitating the usage of antennas or radio dishes. Because infrared light is absorbed by atmospheric water and carbon dioxide, satellites are necessary to record much of the infrared spectrum, even though the technology is comparable to that used in optical spectroscopy.

A prism and photographic plates were used in traditional spectroscopy. Modern spectroscopy disperses light using diffraction gratings, which are then projected onto CCDs (Charge Coupled Devices) similar to those found in digital cameras.

Planets, asteroids, and comets all reflect their parent stars' light while also emitting their own. Most of the emission from colder objects, such as solar-system planets and asteroids, occurs at infrared wavelengths that can't be seen but can be studied using spectrometers. Further emission and absorption at certain wavelengths in the gas occurs for objects surrounded by gas, such as comets and planets with atmospheres, imprinting the gas spectra on the spectrum of the solid object.

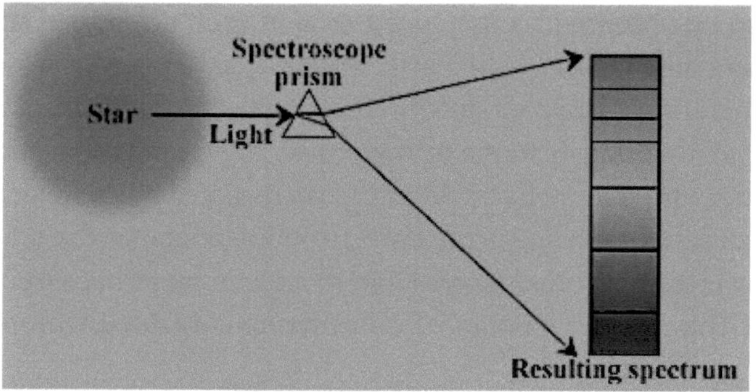

Spectroscopy technique of splitting light into its constituent wavelengths

The absorption bands in the reflected light of a planet are caused by minerals in the rocks present in rocky planets, or by elements and molecules present in the atmosphere. Over 3,500 exoplanets have been identified to date. Hot Jupiters and Earth-like planets are examples of this. Alkali metals, water vapour, carbon monoxide, carbon dioxide, and methane have all been identified via spectroscopy.Comet spectra include reflected solar spectrum from dusty clouds encircling the comet, as well as emission lines from gaseous atoms and molecules fluorescing due to sunlight and/or chemical processes.

Pairs of stars can orbit each other in the same way that planets can orbit each other. Visual binaries are binary stars that may be spotted around each other using a telescope. However, some binary stars are too close together to resolve. When seen through a spectrometer, the spectrums of these two stars will be combined to form a composite spectra. When the stars are of similar luminosity and spectral class, the composite spectrum becomes easier to identify.The radial velocity of spectroscopic binaries can also be observed; as they orbit around each other, one star may come closer to the Earth while the other travels away, generating a Doppler shift in the composite spectrum.

Many other features of the observable population, such as age and interstellar reddening, are revealed by the overall structure of the spectrum .Spectroscopy is one of the most powerful instruments available to astronomers because of the tremendous amount of information contained within a single spectrum.

THEORETICAL ASTRONOMY

CHAPTER SEVEN

THEORETICAL ASTRONOMY

The use of analytical and computational models based on physics and chemistry concepts to describe and explain celestial objects and phenomena is known as theoretical astronomy.When astronomers observe an event predicted by a model, they might choose amongst various alternate or conflicting theories to describe the phenomenon. Observational astronomy, astrometry, astrochemistry, and astrophysics all contribute to theoretical astronomy.

Because the effects of general relativity are weak for most celestial objects, much theoretical astronomy relies on Newton's theory of gravitation. Theoretical astronomy has largely focused on examining the seemingly complex yet periodic motions of celestial objects, rather than attempting to predict the position, size, and temperature of every object in the cosmos.

The work of Johannes Kepler (1571–1630), particularly Kepler's laws, is often seen as the beginning of modern theoretical astronomy. The history of the Solar System's descriptive and theoretical features largely dates from the late fifteenth to the late nineteenth centuries.

Computational tools for modelling star and galaxy development and celestial mechanics were first used in astronomy. Not only must the mathematical expression be reasonably accurate in theoretical astronomy, but it should preferably exist in a form that allows for further mathematical analysis when applied to specific issues.

Astronomy's goal is to learn about the physics and chemistry that underpin cosmic occurrences in order to improve our understanding of both the universe and these sciences.

Astrochemistry is the study of the abundance and interactions of chemical elements and molecules in space, as well as their interaction with radiation. It is a combination of astronomy and chemistry. The origin, atomic and chemical composition, history, and fate of molecular gas clouds are of particular interest since solar systems are formed from these clouds.

Astronomy has aided in the advancement of our knowledge of physics. Physics has aided the understanding of astronomical phenomena, while astronomy has aided the understanding of physical phenomena.Stellar photospheres, stellar atmospheres, the solar atmosphere, planetary atmospheres, gaseous nebulae, nonstationary stars, and the interstellar medium are among the topics that are frequently studied using theoretical physics . The interior structure of stars is given special study.

Theoretical astronomers use a number of methods, including analytical models such as polytropes to mimic a star's behaviour and computational numerical simulations. Each has some benefits. Analytical models of a process are often more effective in revealing the heart of the matter. Numerical models can uncover occurrences and consequences that would otherwise go undetected.

Astronomy theorists strive to develop theoretical models and determine their observational implications. This aids observers in looking for facts that can be used to reject a model or in deciding between several competing hypotheses.

Theorists also attempt to create or change models in order to include new data. In line with the overall scientific method, the general trend in the case of an inconsistency is to try to make minimum changes to the model to fit the data. A substantial volume of conflicting data over time may lead to the complete abandoning of a model in some situations.

Topics studied by theoretical astronomers include:

- Stellar dynamics and evolution;
- Galaxy formation;
- Large-scale structure of matter in the Universe;
- Origin of cosmic rays;
- General relativity and physical cosmology, including string cosmology and astroparticle physics.

Astrophysical relativity is a method for determining the properties of large scale objects in which gravitation plays a substantial part in the physical phenomena studied, as well as the foundation for black hole astrophysics and gravitational wave research. The Big Bang, cosmic inflation, dark matter, and fundamental theories of physics are among the generally accepted and studied astronomical ideas and models presently incorporated in the Lambda-CDM model.

Although most of the mathematics required to comprehend the data obtained through astronomical observation comes from physics, there are some unique requirements arising from situations in which mathematics is intertwined with phenomena for which there is insufficient physics to explain the observations. Math that astronomers are use include Trigonometry,Conics,Differential and integral calculus,Differential geometry,Statistics and probabilities

The apparent motions of the planets were first understood geometrically and independently of gravity in terms of epicycles, which are the summation of many circular motions. This type of theory predicted the courses of the planets reasonably well until Johannes Kepler demonstrated that planet motions were elliptical motions.

Dark matter and dark energy are the current leading topics in astronomy,as their discovery and controversy originated during the study of the galaxies.

ARCHAEOASTRONOMY

CHAPTER EIGHT

ARCHAEOASTRONOMY

The interdisciplinary or multidisciplinary study of how humans in the past "comprehended the phenomena in the sky, how they utilised these phenomena, and what role the sky played in their cultures" is known as archaeoastronomy . Archaeoastronomy is not the study of ancient astronomy, according to Clive Ruggles, because current astronomy is a scientific field, whereas archaeoastronomy analyses symbolically rich cultural interpretations of events in the sky by other cultures.

Ethnoastronomy, the anthropological study of skywatching in contemporary societies, is frequently associated with it. Historical astronomy, the use of historical records of heavenly events to solve astronomical difficulties, and the history of astronomy, which employs written records to evaluate past astronomical practise, are also closely related to archaeoastronomy.

Archaeology, anthropology, astronomy, statistics and probability, and history are all used in archaeoastronomy to find evidence of historical behaviours. Because these methodologies are so diverse and employ data from so many various sources, archaeoastronomers have struggled for a long time to integrate them into a coherent argument. Landscape archaeology and cognitive archaeology both benefit from archaeoastronomy.Archaeoastronomy has long been thought of as an interdisciplinary topic that studies the astronomies of other cultures using written and unwritten data. As a result, it can be seen as bridging the gap between astroarchaeology (an obsolete term for studies that derive astronomical information from the alignments of ancient architecture and landscapes), history of astronomy which focuses on written textual evidence, and ethnoastronomy which focuses on oral tradition which draws on the ethnohistorical record and contemporary ethnographic studies.

Material evidence and its relationship to the sky can illustrate how a larger landscape might be integrated into beliefs about natural cycles, such as Mayan astronomy and agriculture. Studies of the cosmic order encoded in settlement routes are another example of how cognition and landscape have come together.

All cultures and time periods can benefit from archaeoastronomy. Although the meanings of the sky differ from culture to culture, there are scientific tools that may be used to investigate old beliefs across cultures. Perhaps it was the necessity to reconcile the social and scientific sides of archaeoastronomy that caused Clive Ruggles to define it as "a field with high-quality academic study on one end and wild speculation bordering on madness on the other".

Elizabeth Chesley Baity coined the word archaeoastronomy in 1973 (after Euan MacKie's idea), but it could be considerably older as a field of study, depending on how archaeoastronomy is defined. Heinrich Nissen, who worked in the mid-nineteenth century, was perhaps the first archaeoastronomer, according to Clive Ruggles. Norman Lockyer, according to Rolf Sinclair, might be termed the "father of archaeoastronomy" because of his work in the late 19th and early 20th centuries. "...the genesis and present blooming of archaeoastronomy must definitely lie in the work of Alexander Thom in Britain between the 1930s and the 1970s," says Euan MacKie.The work of engineer Alexander Thom and astronomer Gerald Hawkins, who argued that Stonehenge was a Neolithic computer in the 1960s, sparked renewed interest in ancient structures' astronomical aspects.

Observers and practitioners of archaeoastronomy take varied approaches to the topic. Others link archaeoastronomy to the history of science, either in terms of a culture's observations of nature and the conceptual framework they devised to impose order on those observations, or in terms of the political motivations that drove particular historical actors to employ certain astronomical concepts or techniques.

Professional archaeologists' reactions to archaeoastronomy have been very divided. Some voiced bewilderment or even animosity, ranging from the archaeological mainstream's rejection of what they viewed as an archaeoastronomical fringe to a mismatch between archaeologists' cultural focus and early archaeoastronomers' quantitative focus.

Green archaeoastronomy is named after the book Archaeoastronomy in the Old World, which has a green cover. It is mostly based on statistics, and it is especially useful for prehistoric sites where social evidence is sparse in comparison to the historic period. During his comprehensive studies of British megalithic sites, Alexander Thom devised the basic methodologies.

Thom was interested in seeing if prehistoric peoples used high-accuracy astronomy. He claimed that observers could estimate dates in the year to a specific day using horizon astronomy. Finding a location where the sunset into a notch in the horizon on a specified date was required for the observation. A common motif is a mountain that blocks the Sun yet allows the tiniest percentage to re-emerge on the opposite side on the appropriate day, creating a 'double sunset.'

He surveyed hundreds of stone rows and circles to put his theory to the test. Any individual alignment could indicate a direction by chance, but he hoped to establish that the distribution of alignments as a whole was not random, implying that at least some of the alignments were oriented with astronomical design. His findings suggested that the year could be divided into eight, sixteen, or even thirty-two roughly equal sections. The mediaeval Celtic calendar was based on the two solstices, two equinoxes, and four cross-quarter days midway between a solstice and an equinox. While not all of the conclusions were accepted, it had a lasting impact on archaeoastronomy, particularly in Europe.

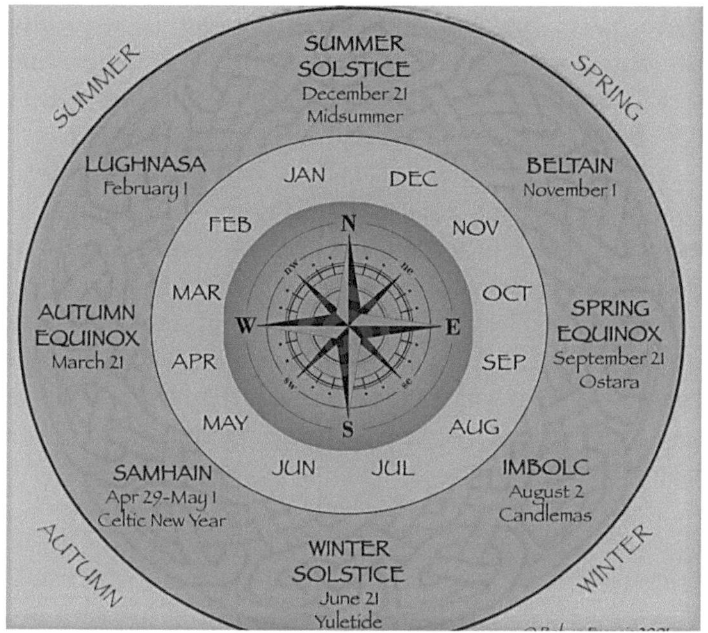

Celtic eightfold year transposed to Southern Hemisphere seasons

A more serious criticism of Green archaeoastronomy is that, while it can answer if there was likely to be an interest in astronomy in the past, it struggles to explain why people would be interested, making it of limited help to individuals researching ancient societies.

Brown archaeoastronomy- Brown archaeoastronomy has been identified as being closer to the history of astronomy or cultural history, insofar as it draws on historical and ethnographic records to enrich its understanding of early astronomies and their relationships to calendars and ritual, as opposed to the largely alignment-oriented statistically led methods of green archaeoastronomy.Brown archaeoastronomy is frequently associated with studies of astronomy in the Americas due to the numerous records of native traditions and beliefs kept by Spanish chroniclers and anthropological scholars.

Chichen Itza is a well-known site where historical sources have been used to explain the site. Rather of evaluating the site to determine which targets appear to be popular, archaeoastronomers looked at anthropological sources to understand what aspects of the sky were important to the Mayans, then looked for archaeological parallels. The Mayan fascination with the planet Venus is one example that might have gone unnoticed if not for historical documents.

Archaeological site at Chichén Itzá in the Yucatan Peninsula, Mexico

The Dresden codex, which contains tables with information regarding Venus's sightings in the sky, attests to this interest. Venus was identified with Quetzalcoatl or

Xolotl, therefore these cycles would have had astrological and religious importance. Architectural characteristics associated with Venusian settings have been found in Chichen Itza, Uxmal, and maybe other Mesoamerican sites.

The brown methodology's strength is that it may investigate astronomies that are not visible to statistical analysis, as the Incas' astronomy exemplifies. Ceques, radial highways radiating from Cusco's capital, were used to conceptually partition the Inca empire. As a result, there are alignments in all directions, implying that there is little astronomical significance.

However, ethnohistorical records show that the various directions do have cosmological and astronomical significance, with different points in the landscape being significant at different times of the year. Archaeoastronomy arose from the history of astronomy in eastern Asia, and most archaeoastronomy is concerned with finding tangible correlations to the historical record.

The study of alignments is a common source of data for archaeoastronomy. This is founded on the premise that an archaeological site's alignment axis is meaningfully directed towards an astronomical target. Green archaeoastronomers tend to prove that alignments are unlikely to have been selected by chance, usually by demonstrating common patterns of alignment at multiple sites. Brown archaeoastronomers may justify this assumption by reading historical or ethnographic sources, whereas brown archaeoastronomers may justify this assumption by reading historical or ethnographic sources.

The use of calendars-The requirement for an accurate calendar for agricultural purposes is a popular explanation for the necessity for astronomy. Old literature such as Hesiod's Works and Days, an ancient farming manual, appear to partially validate this: to determine the seasons, astronomical measurements are combined with ecological indicators such as bird migrations. According to ethnoastronomical studies of the Hopi people of the southwest United States, they meticulously studied the Sun's rising and setting positions to determine the best times to plant crops.

The Tzolk'in calendar of the Maya culture of pre-Columbian Mesoamerica, which has a 260-day cycle, is an example of a non-agricultural calendar. This tally is based on an older calendar and can be found all over Mesoamerica. This was part of a larger Maya calendar system that included a series of astronomical observations and ritual cycles. Ancient Greek calendars are another unusual calendar. Starting with the New Moon, these were ostensibly lunar.

Another reason for observing the sky is to have a better understanding of and explanation for the universe. In these societies, myth was a mechanism for accomplishing this, and the explanations, while not up to modern scientific standards, are cosmologies. The Incas built their empire in such a way that it demonstrated their cosmology. Cusco, the empire's capital, was at its heart and was linked to it by ceques, or essentially straight lines extending outward from the centre. These ceques linked the empire's heart to the empire's four suyus, or areas designated by their distance from Cusco. The idea of a quartered cosmos is widespread in the Andes.

Giorgio de Santillana, a professor of history of science in the Massachusetts Institute of Technology's School of Humanities, and Hertha von Dechend believed that the old mythological stories passed down from antiquity were accurate depictions of celestial cosmology dressed up in stories to aid oral transmission. Ancient stories' turmoil, demons, and violence are symbolic of the forces that shape each age. Ancient myths, they argued, were the remnants of preliterate astronomy that had been lost with the emergence of Greco-Roman civilisation.

Astrotheology, astral mysticism, astral religion, astral or stellar theology, also known as astral or star worship, is the worship of the stars as deities, either individually or collectively as the night sky, the planets, and other heavenly bodies, or the association of deities with heavenly bodies. Astral cults are a term used in anthropological literature to describe these types of practises. Sun gods and moon gods are the most common examples of this in polytheistic systems around the world. Mercury, Venus, Mars, Jupiter, and Saturn, for example, were associated with deities in Babylonian, and so in Greco-Roman religion. Personifications of astronomical phenomena such as lunar eclipses, planetary alignments, and apparent interactions of planetary bodies with stars may also be regarded gods, goddesses, and demons.

Cultural astronomy, sometimes known as "cultural astronomy," is the study of "the multiplicity of ways in which cultures, both ancient and modern, interpret celestial objects and integrate them into their vision of the world." As a result, it covered a wide range of interdisciplinary subjects that looked into the astronomies of modern and ancient societies and cultures. It arose from the interdisciplinary fields of archaeoastronomy and ethnoastronomy the reconstruction of lifeways, astronomical techniques, and rituals using astronomy, textual scholarship, ethnology, and the interpretation of ancient iconography.Celestial artefacts were associated with gods and spirits in ancient cultures. Rain, drought, seasons, and tides were all linked to these things and their movements. It is widely assumed that the first astronomers were priests who saw celestial objects and events as divine manifestations, thus early astronomy's connection to what is now known as astrology.

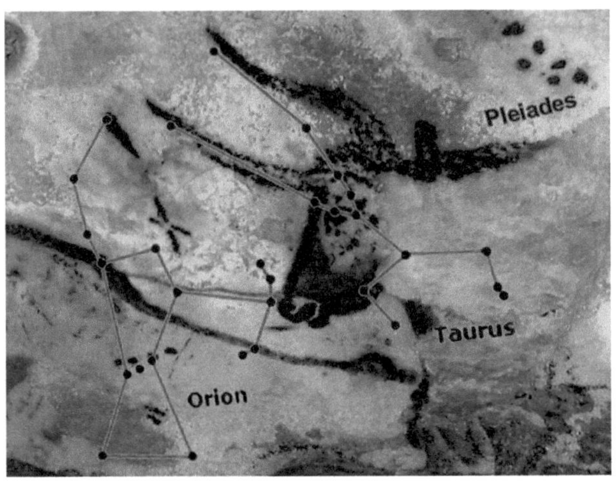

Lascaux Cave, France, showing the supposed star chart panel of Taurus

The earliest known star chart could be found in a 32,500-year-old carved ivory mammoth tusk (resembling the constellation Orion). It's also been hypothesised that a pictorial representation of the Pleiades, the Summer Triangle, and the Northern Crown could be seen on the wall of the Lascaux caves in France, which date from 33,000 to 10,000 years ago. Ancient structures with astronomical alignments most likely served astronomical, religious, and societal purposes.

Cultural astronomy is also linked to historical astronomy, which examines historical astronomical data, history of astronomy, which entails the understanding, study, and evolution of the discipline of astronomy over the course of human knowledge, and history of astrology, which entails the investigation of astrology-astronomy relationships.Examples include

Astronomy in Ancient Greece
Aboriginal astronomy in Australia
Astronomy in Babylonia
Astronomy in China
Astronomy in Egypt
Astronomy in Hebrew
Astronomy in India
Astronomy in the Maya culture
Astronomy in the Inuit culture
Astronomy in Persia
Folk astronomy in Serbia
Astronomy in Tibet
Astronomy in the Islamic world of the Middle Ages

The Ancient Greeks advanced astronomy to a high level of sophistication, treating it as a branch of mathematics. Eudoxus of Cnidus and Callippus of Cyzicus constructed the first geometrical, three-dimensional models to explain the apparent motion of the planets in the 4th century BC. Their models were based on Earth-centered nested homocentric spheres. Heraclides Ponticus, a younger contemporary, suggested that the Earth rotates about its axis.

The Antikythera mechanism, a 150–100 BC Greek astronomical observational system for calculating the movements of the Sun and Moon, and probably the planets, was the first ancestor of an astronomical computer. It was discovered in an old shipwreck between the Greek islands of Kythera and Crete, off the coast of Antikythera. The gadget was noteworthy for its use of a differential gear, which was previously thought to have been invented in the 16th century, as well as the miniaturisation and complexity of its parts,which were comparable to those of an 18th-century clock.

The ancient kingdoms of Sumer, Assyria, and Babylonia were located in Mesopotamia, the "region between the rivers" Tigris and Euphrates, where the origins of Western astronomy may be traced. Around 3500–3000 BC, the Sumerians developed a writing system known as cuneiform. Our understanding of Sumerian astronomy is based on the earliest Babylonian star catalogues, which date back to around 1200 BC.

Babylonian records are the first to show that celestial occurrences are periodic and that mathematics may be used to forecast them. The application of mathematics to the fluctuation in the length of daylight across a solar year is documented on tablets dating back to the Old Babylonian period. The Enma Anu Enlil is a series of cuneiform tablets that record centuries of Babylonian observations of astronomical events. Tablet 63 of the Enma Anu Enlil, the Venus tablet of Ammi-saduqa, is the earliest evidence that the phenomena of a planet were recognised as periodic. It lists the first and last visible risings of Venus over a period of about 21 years and is the earliest evidence that the phenomena of a planet were recognised as periodic.

The MUL.APIN comprises star and constellation catalogues, as well as schemes for predicting heliacal risings and planet sets, lengths of daylight measured by a water clock, gnomon, shadows, and intercalations, and lengths of daylight measured by a water clock, gnomon, shadows, and intercalations. The Babylonian GU book uses stars in'strings' that run along declination circles to measure right-ascensions or time intervals, as well as zenith stars, which are likewise separated by right-ascension discrepancies.

Astronomy was utilised to establish calendars in the Indian subcontinent during the Indus Valley Civilization period in the third millennium BCE. The Vedanga Jyotisha, which dates from the Vedic period, is the oldest known Indian astronomical text due to the lack of written documentation left by the Indus Valley civilization.

The Vedanga Jyotisha is attributed to Lagadha and has an internal date of around 1350 b.c. It describes instructions for tracking the Sun and Moon's motions for ritual reasons. It exists in two recensions, one from the Rig Veda and the other from the Yajur Veda.

A yuga, or "period," has 5 solar years, 67 lunar sidereal cycles, 1,830 days, 1,835 sidereal days, and 62 synodic months, according to the Vedanga Jyotisha.

Aryabhata (476–550) proposed a computational system based on a planetary model in which the Earth was assumed to be spinning on its axis and the periods of the planets were given with respect to the Sun in his magnum opus Aryabhatiya (499).

Many astronomical constants, such as the periods of the planets, the times of solar and lunar eclipses, and the Moon's instantaneous velocity, were precisely determined by him. Varahamihira, Brahmagupta, and Bhaskara II were early adherents of Aryabhata's model.

During the Shunga Empire, astronomy advanced, and numerous star catalogues were published. The Shunga period is regarded as India's "Golden Age of Astronomy." It saw the evolution of calculations for the motions and positions of several planets, as well as their rising and setting, conjunctions, and eclipse calculations.

By the sixth century, Indian astronomers believed that comets were heavenly bodies that re-appeared on a regular basis. The astronomers Varahamihira and Bhadrabahu articulated this viewpoint in the 6th century, while the 10th-century astronomer Bhattotpala catalogued the names and estimated periods of other comets.

Nilakantha Somayaji developed his own computational system for a partially heliocentric planetary model in his Aryabhatiyabhasya, a commentary on Aryabhata's Aryabhatiya, in which Mercury, Venus, Mars, Jupiter, and Saturn orbit the Sun, which in turn orbits the Earth, similar to the Tychonic system later proposed by Tycho Brahe in the late 16th century. Nilakantha's system, on the other hand, was theoretically more efficient than the Tychonic system since it accurately calculated the equation of the centre and Mercury and Venus' latitudinal motion.

The Egyptian pyramids' perfect orientation is a permanent demonstration of the great level of technical proficiency in observing the heavens acquired in the third millennium BC. The Pyramids were orientated towards the pole star, which at the time was Thuban, a dim star in the constellation of Draco, due to the precession of the equinoxes.

Pole star, which at the time was Thuban, a dim star in the constellation of Draco, due to the precession of the equinoxes.

The Great Temple of Karnak was positioned on the rising of the midwinter Sun, according to an evaluation of the site of the temple of Amun-Re at Karnak that took into account the shift in the obliquity of the ecliptic over time.

Astronomy was used extensively in religious matters to determine the dates of festivals and the hours of the night. The titles of various temple books that chronicle the movements and phases of the sun, moon, and stars have been preserved. The rising of Sirius (Egyptian: Sopdet, Greek: Sothis) at the start of the flood was a crucial date to mark on the annual calendar.

China was the birthplace of East Asian astronomy. During the Warring States period, the solar term was completed. East Asia was exposed to Chinese astronomy for the first time.Astronomy has a long history in China. From around the 6th century BC until the introduction of Western astronomy and the telescope in the 17th century, detailed records of astronomical observations were kept. Chinese astronomers were able to predict eclipses with great accuracy.

The objective of much of early Chinese astronomy was to keep track of time. The Chinese employed a lunisolar calendar, but because the Sun's and Moon's cycles differed, astronomers frequently created new calendars and made observations for this reason.

Astrology included the practise of astrological divination. Astronomers kept a close eye on "guest stars" that emerged out of nowhere among the fixed stars. In the Astrological Annals of the Houhanshu in 185 AD, they were the first to chronicle a supernova. In addition, the supernova that generated the Crab Nebula in 1054 was an example of a "guest star" noticed by Chinese astronomers, despite the fact that it was not documented by their European counterparts.

In modern astronomical investigations, ancient astronomical records of occurrences such as supernovae and comets are occasionally employed.Gan De, a Chinese astronomer, created the world's first star list in the 4th century BC.

The study of the Moon, planets, Milky Way, Sun, and celestial phenomena by the Precolumbian Maya Civilization of Mesoamerica is known as Maya astronomy. The Classic Maya, in instance, established some of the world's most precise pre-telescope astronomy, supported by their fully developed writing system and positional numeric system, both of which are Mesoamerican natives.

Many astronomical phenomena were comprehended by the Classic Maya: for example, their estimate of the length of the synodic month was more precise than Ptolemy's, and their computation of the length of the tropical solar year was more correct than the Spanish when they came. Many Maya temples include characteristics that are oriented toward cosmic events.

Maya astronomy was founded on the observation of the azimuths of the rising and setting of heavenly bodies with the naked eye. The alignment and planning of cities was frequently done in accordance with celestial routes and events. The Maya also thought that the alignment of the planets and stars might reveal gods' intentions and acts.Many wells in Mayan ruins served as observatories for the sun's zenithal passage.The El Caracol at Chichen Itza is one of the most researched Mayan astronomy sites. The Caracol is a year-round observatory that follows the journey of Venus.

Many almanacks and tables in the Maya codices describe the solstices and equinoxes. The Dresden Codex contains three seasonal tables and four related almanacks. The Madrid Codex has five solar almanacks, and the Paris Codex may contain one as well. Many of them date from the second half of the ninth century and the first part of the tenth.

The Dresden Codex, the great Maya book of the stars

The Maya had a good understanding of the solstices and equinoxes. Building alignments are a good example of this. The zenithal passing days were more essential to them. Twice a year, the Sun passes directly overhead in the Tropics. Many Mayan temples are known to have been built to observe this. The observatory at Xochicalco is an example of such a temple. The observatory is a hole in the roof underground room.

The sun would directly illuminate a depiction of the sun on the floor on two days of the year, May 15 and July 29. Except for a few unusual year bearing systems, Munro S. Edmonson researched 60 mesoamerican calendars and found remarkable similarity in the calendars.In opposition to the yearly motion of the Sun along the ecliptic, the equinoxes travel westward along the ecliptic relative to the fixed stars, returning to the same place every 26,000 years.The Dresden codex's "Serpent Numbers," on pages 61–69, is a table of dates written in the coils of undulating serpents. Beyer was the first to realise that the Serpent Series is based on a rather large distance number of 1.18.1.8.0.16 (5,482,096 days - nearly 30,000 years).

Grofe argues that this interval is near to a whole multiple of the sidereal year, bringing the sun back to the exact same position against the backdrop of stars.Along the ecliptic, the Maya identified 13 constellations. These are the contents of a Paris Codex almanack. Each of these was linked to a certain animal. These animal depictions appear in two Madrid Codex almanacks, where they are linked to other astronomical occurrences such as eclipses and Venus, as well as Haab ceremonies.

The study of famous landmarks, historic sculptures, and historical temples allows us to have a deeper understanding of our forefathers' symbolic contact with the sky above. The new study emphasises active collaboration between experts and amateurs from various backgrounds and cultures. As a result of their collaboration, archaeoastronomy has grown to incorporate associated interests in ancient and native calendar systems, as well as time and space conceptions.

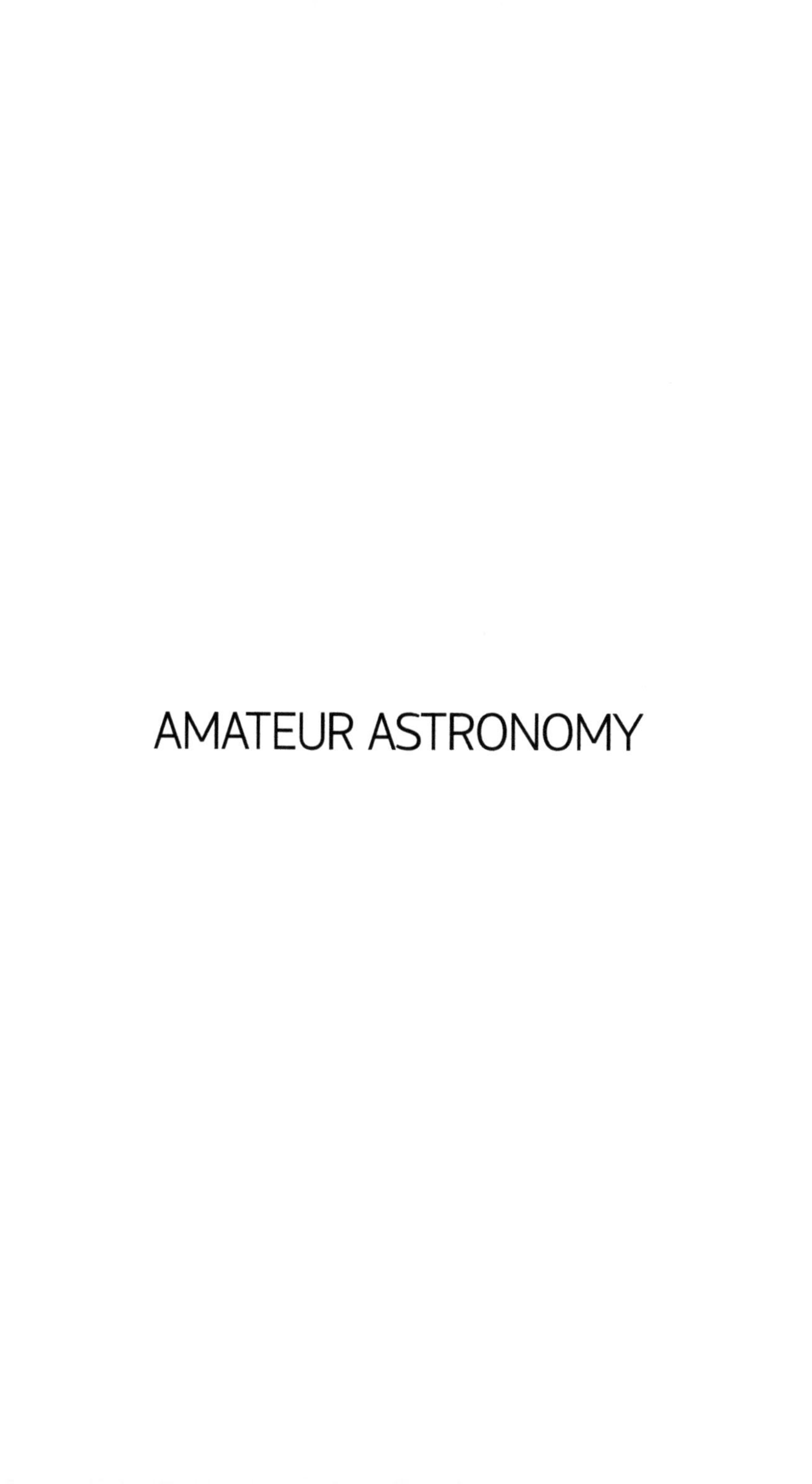

AMATEUR ASTRONOMY

CHAPTER NINE

AMATEUR ASTRONOMY

Amateur astronomy is a hobby in which people enjoy looking at or photographing celestial objects in the sky with their naked eyes, binoculars, or telescopes. Some amateur astronomers contribute to scientific studies even if it is not their primary purpose.

Objects monitored include variable stars,double stars,sunspots,or occultations of stars by the Moon or asteroids and also transient astronomical events, such as comets,galactic novaeor supernovae in other galaxies are also viewed.

People enjoy looking at or photographing celestial objects

Many amateur astronomers have studied the sky throughout history; nevertheless, professional astronomy has emerged as a distinct activity from amateur astronomy and related pursuits since the turn of the twentieth century.

Amateur astrophotography is a form of amateur astronomy that involves photographing the night sky. With the emergence of significantly more user-friendly technology, such as digital cameras, DSLR cameras, and relatively complex purpose-built high-quality CCD cameras, astronomy has grown more popular. The majority of amateur astronomers work with visible wavelengths, although a small percentage experiment with wavelengths that are not visible. Grote Reber, an amateur astronomer who built the first purpose-made radio telescope in the late 1930s to follow up on Karl Jansky's discovery of radio wavelength emissions from space, was an early pioneer of radio astronomy. The use of infrared filters on traditional telescopes, as well as the use of radio telescopes, are examples of non-visual amateur astronomy.

Amateur astrophotography -Horseshoe Nebula

Some amateur astronomers build their own radio telescopes, while others use radio telescopes that were designed for astronomical study but have since been made available to amateurs.Amateur astronomers examine the sky with a variety of instruments, depending on their interests and resources. To study light from the sky in both the visual and non-visual parts of the spectrum, methods include simply looking at the night sky with the naked eye, using binoculars, and using a variety of optical telescopes of varying power and quality, as well as additional sophisticated equipment, such as cameras. Commercial telescopes are available, both new and old, although amateur astronomers frequently construct their own bespoke telescopes.

Over time, more specialised and powerful equipment is acquired by specialised and experienced amateur astronomers. Amateur astronomers also employ star charts, which can range from simple planispheres to complex charts of extremely particular portions of the night sky, depending on their experience and aims. Amateur astronomers have access to and use a variety of astronomy software, including sky mapping software, astrophotography software, observation scheduling software, and software to do various computations related to celestial events.

Amateur astronomers frequently keep logs of their observations, which are usually in the form of an observing log.Observing logs normally keep track of which items were seen when and when they were seen, as well as the details that were seen. Sketching is sometimes employed in logs, and more recently, photographic records of observations have been used. Individuals have created a great number of web sites about their photographs and equipment due to the popularity of imaging among amateurs.

Although amateur astronomy employs a variety of approaches, the majority are variants on a few key techniques. Amateur astronomers often utilise low-tech equipment such as binoculars or a manually operated telescope to do star hopping. It entails locating known landmark stars using maps (or memory) and "hopping" between them, frequently with the use of a finderscope. Star hopping is a popular strategy for locating objects that are close to naked-eye stars due to its simplicity.

Telescope mounts with setting circles, which assist with pointing telescopes to known locations in the sky that contain objects of interest, and GOTO telescopes, which are fully automated telescopes capable of locating objects on demand, are more advanced means of locating objects in the sky.

Many specialised apps have sprung out as a result of the introduction of mobile applications for usage on smartphones. These apps allow users to quickly discover astronomical objects of interest in the sky by just pointing their smartphone device in that direction. These apps make use of the phone's built-in hardware, such as the GPS and gyroscope. For rapid reference, useful information about the pointed object is presented, such as astronomical coordinates, the object's name, its constellation, and so on.

Since the 1980s, as technology has advanced and prices have decreased, GOTO telescopes have become increasingly popular. The user often enters the name of the item of interest into these computer-driven telescopes, and the mechanics of the telescope automatically steer the telescope towards that item. For amateur astronomers interested in study, they have numerous obvious advantages. GOTO telescopes, for example, are faster than star hopping at locating objects of interest, allowing more time to analyse the object. GOTO also enables manufacturers to include equatorial tracking onto mechanically simpler alt-azimuth telescope mounts, resulting in a lower-cost product.

"Remote Telescope" astronomy is now a viable means for amateur astronomers not aligned with major telescope facilities to participate in research and deep sky imaging, thanks to the development of fast Internet in the late twentieth century, as well as advances in computer controlled telescope mounts and CCD cameras. This allows anyone to operate a telescope from afar in a dark environment. CCD cameras allow the spectator to see through the telescope. The digital data captured by the telescope is then sent via the Internet and displayed to the user.

Amateur astronomers are frequently involved in activities such as tracking asteroids, monitoring the brightness of variable stars and supernovae, and watching occultations to estimate the form of asteroids and the terrain on the Moon's visible edge as seen from Earth. Amateur astronomers can measure the light spectrum radiated from astronomical objects with more advanced equipment, which is still inexpensive in contrast to professional sets, and can yield high-quality scientific data if the measurements are done properly.

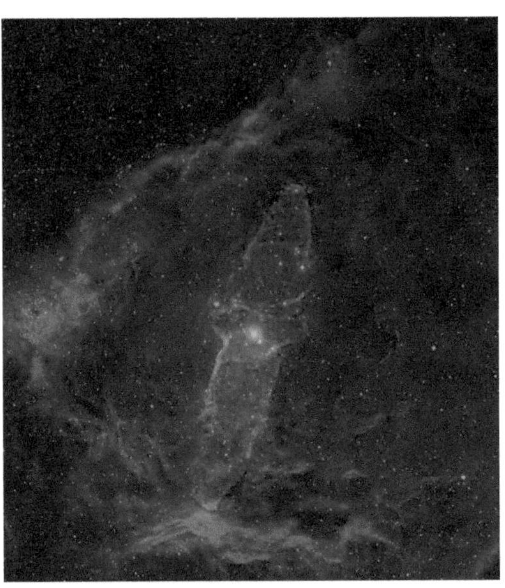

The Giant Squid Nebula, or "Ou 4" is named after its discoverer: Nicolas Outters- An Amateur astronomer and astrophotographer

There are several amateur astronomical societies around the world that serve as a gathering place for amateur astronomy enthusiasts. Major national or worldwide societies usually have their own journal or newsletter, and some host big multi-day gatherings similar to scientific conferences or conventions. They might also feature sections dedicated to specific themes like lunar observation or amateur telescope building.

The majority of amateur astronomers‘ scientific contributions are in the domain of data collecting. This is especially true when a large number of amateur astronomers using small telescopes outperform the relatively small number of large telescopes available to professional astronomers.

Unlike professional astronomers, many amateur astronomers do not pursue scientific study as their primary purpose. However, work of scientific significance is conceivable, and many amateur astronomers successfully add to professional astronomers' knowledge base. Astronomy is occasionally marketed as one of the only sciences in which amateurs can still contribute useful data. The Astronomical Society of the Pacific awards Amateur Achievement Awards each year to amateurs who have made major contributions to astronomy.

Current And Open Research Areas In Astronomy

Observational Astronomy

- Observational/experimental studies of gravitational waves, dark matter and neutrinos
- Scientific planning for future telescopes and instruments
- Multi-wavelength observations of Black Holes and Neutron Stars
- Optical standard star photometry
- Gamma-ray bursts, supernovae, novae
- Instrumental and observational aspects of infrared, X-ray and gamma-ray astronomy,
- Instrumental and observational projects in optical, infrared and millimetre astronomy,

Astrophysics

- Large-scale structure of the Universe
- Cosmology and the Distant Universe.
- Nuclear and particle astrophysics.
- Supernova physics.
- Astrophysical fluid dynamics.
- High-energy astrophysics.
- Disks and Jets.
- Radiative processes.
- Structure, formation and evolution of galaxies.
- Gravitational lensing.
- Structure and evolution of stars .
- Physical and early universe cosmology.
- Accretion phenomena.

- Extreme Physics and Astrophysics of Compact Objects,
- Galaxies Across the Universe.
- Solar Physics
- Black Holes and Neutron Stars,
- Computational Astrophysics

Planetary Science

- Planetary Geology and Surface Processes
- Impact Cratering
- Planetary Remote Sensing and Spectroscopy
- Geochemistry, Petrology and Mineralogy
- Planetary Interiors and Geophysics
- Planetary Atmospheres
- Lunar Science and Exploration
- Asteroids and Other Small Bodies
- Icy Satellites
- Meteorites and Sample Analysis
- Interplanetary Dust and Presolar Grains

Astrobiology

- Origins of organic compounds in space
- Rock-water-carbon interactions
- Organic synthesis on Earth, and steps to life
- Life and habitability
- Biosignatures as facilitating life detection
- Life of Plants in Space
- Redesigning plants to support space exploration
- Sources of organic compounds
- Origin and early evolution of life
- Life beyond Earth

Astro chemitsry

- Chemistry of protoplanetary disks.
- Formation of organic molecules in space
- Molecular millimeter spectroscopy
- Complex organic molecules in different sources in the interstellar medium
- Complex organic moleculesprotoplanetary disks
- Interstellar and circumstellar molecules form and interaction

Astrometry

- Spectra in the atmospheres of exoplanets.
- Spectrographs for the next-generation observatories
- Spectrum of interesting environments, including the regions around newborn star systems
- Celestial mechanics, stellar dynamics and galactic astronomy
- Tracking of near-Earth objects

Theoretical Astrophysics

- Cosmology
- Growth and Evolution of galaxies
- General relativity
- Gravitation,Gravitational waves
- Dark matter
- Quantum black holes.
- Cosmic rays
- Neutron stars and Pulsars
- Star clusters,Quasars

Archaeo Astronomy

- Use of astronomical calendars
- Myth and cosmology
- Astronomy in archaeological record
- Astronomy in beliefs, rituals and symbolism

Amateur Astronomy

- Transit measurements
- Long term variable star observations
- Detection of exoplanets
- Astrophotography

Career In Astronomy

Space exploration and related jobs are a rapidly growing field with a wide range of possible career specialisations.A appropriate education in pure science or engineering areas is required to become a scientist or work in various related fields in Astronomy . Engineers in mechanical, electrical, electronics, and computer science, as well as PhD candidates in astronomy, physics, and mathematics, are sought.

One can contribute to the field of Astronomy by being

- Observational astronomer
- Theoretical astrophysicists
- Astronomy Professor
- Astrophysicist
- Research Consultant
- Research Physicist
- Research Scientist
- Astrobiologist
- Astrochemists
- Aerospace Engineer
- Astronauts
- Geoscientists
- Atmospheric Scientists and Meteorologists
- Research Space Scientist

“*“Exploration is in our nature. We began as wanderers, and we are wanderers still. We have lingered long enough on the shores of the cosmic ocean. We are ready at last to set sail for the stars.”*
— Carl Sagan, Cosmos”

9 798887 493589

Printed by Libri Plureos GmbH in Hamburg,
Germany